THE CLASS OF THE GOLDEN CYCLE

THE CLASS OF THE GOLDEN CYCLE

Now Is the Time to Become an Adept

ELIZABETH CLARE PROPHET

SUMMIT UNIVERSITY PRESS®
Gardiner, Montana

This volume contains all the dictations from The Class of the Golden Cycle conference, October 11–15, 1991, held in New Orleans, Louisiana, as well as the seven dictations delivered August 11, 1991, during the celebration of the thirty-third anniversary of the founding The Summit Lighthouse. These dictations were previously published in *Pearls of Wisdom,* vol. 34, nos. 47–53, 54–59, 61–62 and 64–66. They have been edited by the messenger under the masters' direction for clarity in the written word.

THE CLASS OF THE GOLDEN CYCLE
Now Is the Time to Become an Adept
by Elizabeth Clare Prophet

For information, contact
The Summit Lighthouse, 63 Summit Way, Gardiner, MT 59030 USA
Tel: 1-800-245-5445 or 1 406-848-9500
info@SummitUniversityPress.com
SummitLighthouse.org

Library of Congress Control Number: 2022946530
ISBN: 978-1-60988-426-0 (softbound)
ISBN: 978-1-60988-427-7 (eBook)

SUMMIT UNIVERSITY PRESS®

Note: the original seven dictations delivered in 1958 are published in the 2008 *Pearls of Wisdom,* vol. 51, nos. 9–15

25 24 23 22 1 2 3 4

CONTENTS

FOREWORD

This book records a moment in cosmic history. On October 14, 1991, the ascended master Saint Germain announced the release of a golden cycle of light from the Great Central Sun. He explained that "this is a spiral . . . that shall affect all evolutions of the Matter cosmos according to the cycle of their individual worlds and planes."

This cycle presents a profound opportunity, especially for those who are walking a spiritual path. The Great Divine Director said: "This is the hour when the golden cycle is sent forth from the very heart of Alpha and Omega. The golden cycle comes blazing down the corridor of the centuries, the millenniums, and that golden cycle is a pathway of light on which you can return to God . . . a pathway into infinity."

This cycle is a gift of the quickening of the crown chakra, making available a wisdom intended to propel us and thereby civilization into a self-transcending golden age. The question is, how will we manifest the gift today and ongoing? The ascended masters who spoke at that conference gave many keys to unlock that wisdom, and you will find all their discourses published in this volume.

Serapis Bey and Clara Louise speak of the disciplines of the Ascension Temple and of love as the foundation of the path of the ascension.

Nada speaks of love as meeting every need, as the key to personal and world transformation.

Meta brings a mirror of truth that we might see our divine reality and also see what must be surrendered if we would find our way back to God.

Kuan Yin offers us a cup of mercy, helping us let go of the burdens of the past and find our Real Self.

And the Buddha of the Ruby Ray speaks of the empowerment that we can receive through the path of chelaship at Maitreya's Mystery School.

In all of these releases, the ascended masters show us how to receive the full blessing of this golden cycle from the Central Sun—and it is indeed a great blessing. Saint Germain explains that it brings the opportunity "for you individually to bring forth fruits from your causal body that have not been accessible to you in this life nor in previous lifetimes."

How can we dedicate those fruits in the most meaningful way for the masters? The second section of this book includes dictations from the seven founding masters of The Summit Lighthouse on the inauguration of the second thirty-three-year cycle of their sponsorship of the organization (1991). As we approach the end of that cycle, the Brotherhood's review of the fruit of our dedication will determine the degree to which they can sponsor the organization and its members in the next cycle, from 2024 through 2057.

As you read these words of the masters, may you enter the ongoing spiral of the golden cycle from the sun. And may it lead you all the way Home.

THE EDITORS

CHAPTER 1

Serapis Bey

OBEDIENCE TO LOVE

The Guardian Action of Love

O how wondrous is the path of initiation unto the soul who has accepted the flame of God's own obedient love! For that one has entered into that love which is obedience—truly loving obedience to the divine reason for being.

And that soul has heard the call from Alpha, from Omega, the Father-Mother God, and does no longer tarry in the cups of self-will and human pride and going astray from the very formula of the Law, which is the inner blueprint of one's life.

From the day and the hour that thou dost hear the call of the Guru, beloved—that one who has called thee to the Path, even the path of the living flame of love—*there is no turning back.*

The soul can no longer dally. The flute of Krishna has been heard and the sound of that love does woo the soul above and beyond all earthly loves.

The soul has heard the Call and the soul shall listen with inner ear and inner sight, following the lead and the beckoning of the one who bestows love for the union of all of one's forces.

Yes, beloved, it is one thing to know that obedience to God is achieved only by love and that love is the fulfillment of the law of obedience, and it is another to know the vibration of that love, the quickening of that obedience: the quickening of the power of God that does galvanize all of one's being, repolarizing one's very life to the Polestar of Being, which is the I AM Presence with each one.

God has not left you comfortless.[1] God's comfort is in that Presence and in the living presence of Christ born again and again in every heart until the heart, first the manger and then the palace of light, becomes the dwelling place of both the Father and the Son.[2]

The Father and the Son will teach you the path of love. And when you become immersed in that love in such profound inner joy, there shall come a cessation of idle chatter, of harshness of feelings, sharpness of thoughts—there shall come the softening, the tenderness and the very strength of love.

These changes shall almost surprise you as you become aware that the Third Person of God does enter with Father and Son and your life becomes a walk in the Trinity. And the Holy Spirit shall nevermore go out from that point of the inner light if you keep the love tryst, if you cherish the law of God as the application of his will and rejoice to fulfill it.

How to fulfill the Law, then, if the will be not heard?

It is through the listening by the inner ear, the listening to the voice of God. You must shut out all other sounds so that God's voice resounds within you and the impelling of love teaches the law of right and wrong.

And the Holy Christ Self, so very, very near, does yet remain apart, trying the soul again and again, testing the soul, delivering the soul, refining the soul with Refiner's fire[3] until the soul does wonder, "Shall I forever be remanded to the outer court, outside the door of the heart of my Christ, of my Lord Jesus?"

Again and again true love is tested. Again and again you desire to prove your love even as you are reproved by the one who loves you, the one who is that Guru who does unite you with your twin flame, with Jesus, with Lord Maitreya.

The Teacher comes! The trumpets sound! The Teacher has come to show you the way to answer the beckoning love of Love's own perfect expression of itself.

O beloved, obedience is not hard when you have been touched by divine love in a measure beyond your present comprehension. Love that permeates all being is first of all a forgiving love—God's forgiving of you and your forgiving of all parts of life. Forgiving love is a saturating love, a healing love, a love of resolution.

O soul who art immortal, know that you may wear the swaddling garment of love! You may receive it! For I, Serapis, come as the mediator of that love that may be too tender, almost too profound to receive and contain.

God's love is beyond all of self and selfhood.

What need have you of outer self when you are in the beginning with love and in the ending with love and you are in God and in the heart of God and God is in your heart?

There is nothing you cannot give away, for, beloved, you have the allness of the cosmos. And you know that in the giving of self or possessions (if you have not already given them), you impart some measure of that allness as token to those who are yet in the outer circle and have not entered in to the fullness of that bliss of communion with the Bridegroom, who is Christ the Lord.

O devotees of ascension's flame, you have known the true love of that flame! You have known of Serapis. You have known of the love of twin flames of the fourth ray and you have understood the sound of the flame in the "March Triumphal," in the sweet love call unto the "Celeste Aïda."

Yes, beloved, you have seen in the white fire of Luxor's temple the vision of the merging of the white-fire body of yourself and your twin flame that shall take place at that date when you are summoned to the return of the divine Oneness. You have seen the merging of your causal bodies. You have known the promise of the fulfillment of this path.

Therefore I counsel you, do not desire anything inordinately. Do not entertain any longer inordinate desire, for you remove yourself thereby from the fount of true and living love.

Give obedience in little things, for the little matters must be settled, else they will become big fires out of control. Let the little problems in life be seen as significant* of the larger ones.

---

*indicative

When men ignore the larger problems of a planet in distress for the smaller ones of inconsequence, they surely do suffer: they suffer the loss of vision and experience a failed test in a schoolroom of life. But let not the larger worldview eclipse the affairs of your immediate circle, causing you to abandon the first responsibilities of life.

Thus, from either too close or too distant a view you may miss the point of the practicality denoted by the sand falling in the hourglass, the single grain of sand that you must cast as a diamond ere it fall in that moment of time arrested, eternity waiting, suspension.

How long is the suspension of a single grain of sand?

Does not the sun stand still for the son or the daughter of God who must weigh the factors of time and eternity to make that split-second decision for the right, for the championing of life and truth and honor?

Yes, love is the great synthesizer of all, the fire infolding itself. Love begets love, the many forms of love that all need—from mercy to chastisement, from firmness unto the beauty of star-fire glow.

I AM Serapis in the newness of love and its fulfillment.

I am with you to increase your sense of heaven here below. A circle of light I now draw around you, each one, to extend the borders of your habitation, to magnetize love to your aura that you might become the magnet for love, for giving and receiving love, failing not to remember that love is lost when you disobey the first commandment:

Thou shalt have no other gods before me.[4]

This is the first obedience and the First Love.

Therefore be purged, I say, of lesser loves so that you do not misqualify God's love but that you enter in to it and allow it to translate you again and again and again!

Be willing to be translated day by day, to be transfigured and to know that your loves of yesterday are not sufficient unto your loves of today nor will they suffice unto tomorrow's.

Yes, beloved, love is eternally new as the eternally new springtime, as flowers that come and blossom become immortelles and recycle, passing through time and space again.

O great love of God, as thou hast ordained the cycles in order to give opportunity in this hour to many of thy servants upon earth, so I have come to impress upon both the souls who hear me not through this messenger and those who do (or shall by the recording) that that love is for the fulfilling of the whole law: and when the law of love is fulfilled, opportunity opens. And the opportunity to bear greater love of God is surely an initiation.

Love must be protected by the call to Saint Michael the Archangel. Love must be protected by the use of wisdom, its exercise for the guardian action of love. The power of God must be wooed and won by you that that power, which is endowed with God's will, shall become the fortress for the sealing of love against the hordes of night, who would steal it and pervert it and misqualify the sacred fire and take that divine love to depths where love must not go.

So shall there be unto you an opportunity to be all love. But this love shall not affix itself unto you or your aura until you demonstrate considerable proficiency in holding love's harmony, preferring your calls to Archangel Michael and to the will of God (rather than those to love itself) for the protection of the most precious gift of all cosmos.

God has sent me to you in this hour as your fellow servant and brother that I might express to you this opportunity to hold love's balance. Love presents the greatest of all tests of the seven rays, beloved, simply because the forces of darkness would tear from you in any moment the precious love that is unto you a rare elixir of everlasting life.

Just as soon as you are strengthened in light, light and light, just as soon as you are firmly on the Path, know that God shall give you a portion of love through my hand that will enable you to accelerate on the Path in dimensions beyond all prior attainment.

Thus, know the requirement of such an opportunity and such an initiation. It is the guardian action, *the guardian action of love.* May you know it well and soon come to know yourself in the glass as a true reflection of God's love to all people.

Would you be the smile and the joy and the gift of love, my beloved, in specific, very specific vibration for each one—a precious love that you may impart, which becomes an unguent, truly a balm of healing of old wounds and hurts and separations and losses?

Yes, beloved, you can call to the secret love star. It is the causal body cumulative of all evolutions who have won their victory on your sister star, Venus. This secret love star becomes an action of ruby fire: protecting love, containing love and multiplying your momentum of love that is yours only through the Sacred Heart of Jesus and yours alone in his heart.

Yes, beloved, melt all the world's hate and hate creation with the love of the living Christ Jesus with you and see how the world shall be changed!

I commend you to the first steps of love's obedience. Once you have followed these, you will follow all the rest if you truly love.

In the words of Jesus,[5] may you love one another as I, Serapis, have loved you.

As you have come to our retreat to study, so know that some have done exceptionally well and shall soon enter into new chambers—chambers of advanced initiation.

By the victory of the one, doors are opened to the many. May you contemplate the One and smile the peace of love.

October 11, 1991
New Orleans, Louisiana
Elizabeth Clare Prophet

Serapis Bey is the chohan of the fourth ray (white ray) of purity. Known as the great disciplinarian, Serapis trains candidates for the ascension at his retreat, the Ascension Temple, at Luxor, Egypt. This retreat is in the etheric octave, superimposed over the physical Temple of Luxor on the Nile. Among those attending classes at Luxor are artists, musicians, sculptors, architects, planners, and the most staunch disciples of every ray. Serapis Bey's devotion to the flame of purity is evidenced in his service throughout his embodiments on earth. These include: high priest in the Ascension Temple on Atlantis; Amenhotep III, Egyptian pharaoh (reigned c. 1388–1351 B.C.); Leonidas, king of Sparta (c. 480 B.C.); and Phidias, Greek sculptor (c. 475–425 B.C.). The ascended master Serapis Bey initiates our souls in the flame of God-harmony, charted on the six o'clock line of the cosmic clock under the solar hierarchy of Cancer. His keynote is "Celeste Aïda" by Verdi. The melody of the ascension flame is the "Triumphal March," also by Verdi.

(See *The Masters and Their Retreats,* pp. 330–37; and Serapis Bey, *Dossier on the Ascension.*)

CHAPTER 2

Lady Master Clara Louise

SELF-DISCIPLINE ON THE PATH TO THE ASCENSION

Embody the Flaming Fire of the Saviour's Love

The one who shall abide in the day of the coming of the messenger of God[1] is the initiate who is self-disciplined on the path of the ascension.

Let me hasten to tell you that self-discipline is never rigid nor is it unlawfully proud. It is not accomplished at all by the carnal mind. It is the discipline of the disciple who has first loved, who has placed his head on the breast of Jesus,[2] who has known the heartbeat of the Lord and that tenderness which the human heart can scarcely contain.

Yes, beloved, true self-discipline is never rigidity but it is love fulfilling itself by the intuitive powers of the soul, by the discrimination of the heart, by true discernment of the mind. These are inner qualities of the five secret rays that sensitize even the soul to the understanding that though all the rules be followed, yet without love the disciple cannot succeed.

At the Ascension Temple we find that certain neophytes who are in fear of God instead of in love with God always seek to confine God to a set of rules whereby if they follow those rules, they cannot be denied. Then one day for the class at Luxor all the rules are dropped as though there were no more foundations or pillars in the temple.

Those who have sought to attain by a set of rules, beloved, may at this point suffer temporary insanity or a prolonged lapse of sense of identity. They pale into a fear that is perhaps beyond any fear they have known. All of a sudden they have no moorings, no coordinates. They are as blind men and sense themselves so.

"How shall we fulfill the requirements of the law of Serapis," they complain, "if there be no guidelines?" To which the mentor responds: "It is by the internalization of the flame of love that right action ensues in the Guru-chela relationship."

Therefore, if you have not internalized the Word, the Word incarnate in Jesus Christ, by assimilating his light essence, his Body and his Blood, then the inner standard will not be developed and you can be taken only to that level where there are yet maps and rules that you can lean upon. This is good exercise, beloved, but never true attainment.

Thus, go within. Hear the call of Archangel Michael to seek adeptship[3] and do so. Love on this path is truly a disciplined love.

What is disciplined love?

It is that which moves the pen or the paintbrush, that which designs cathedrals, lays foundations for underwater passageways, mighty ships that sail the seven seas and those that journey beyond the stars. Disciplined love is the foundation of all creativity and accomplishment of design and geometry that sets the pattern of all living.

Undisciplined love is no love at all. Those who prate about love and yet do not know how to hold the strings of love taut or to tune their violins or lutes or harps, these, then, have an incomplete concept of love, which mirrors relativity but not the Absolute.

Pure and simple, absolute love is God in complete manifestation. Relative love is but a turning around of that love to suit the human convenience of being able to talk about love. It is a love that is not from the sacred altars of God but is still the human comprehension of love—of getting, forgiving, seeking recompense, seeking possession or control or favor. These perversions of love are rated as love by many, even as sympathy is sought and expressed as though it were God's love.

The charity and compassion of God sees beyond the centuries, lays foundations, prepares for future generations embodying, knows the whole circle of God's love and where a race must be in a thousand years and will work to see to it that when they arrive at the place, the place will be prepared.

Love is vision. Love is foresight. Love is taking care of details that none other will and therefore the mission should otherwise be lost.

Love is understanding the complexity of the team of lightbearers of an entire cosmos. Imagine this team, of which you are a part. Imagine how the team members have become players on this team. Imagine how they have disciplined self to take care of the details of life that have enabled another to fulfill the divine plan.

Think of a Nada, a Rose of Light, a Lady Master Venus, a Chamuel and Charity. Think of a cosmos of beings of love and the true love your soul longs to be the recipient of—a love that truly loves the Real and forgives the unreal but compels the unreal to rise and rise again and again and again until that rising is perfected in the Sun behind the sun.

O beloved, the path of the fourth ray, which we bring you this night, is a white fire that is so intense that you may not detect the golden pink glow-ray of its aura or the depths of the rose and the ruby within its stalk. Yes, beloved, love comes in all disguises of all the rays yet love is perfected in the white fire of discipleship unto the true self-discipline of the joyous ones.

Seraphim of God have come this night. They come to this city to restore the souls of many who have lost the way for centuries. They have been called by El Morya and the Darjeeling Council. They have come for an infusion of white light that begets all love excelling and excelling.

Many are called to the love feast. Many come at inner levels. May you call for them to be cut free by the seraphim this night to find the living reality of the path of love embodied in the true teachings of Jesus Christ that have been lost. Yes, beloved, many on inner planes cry out to you to call to the angels to cut them free that they might make the same connection to the fount of living love that you have made.

Love is a continuity of being.

What else could sustain you lifetime after lifetime in the imperfected state, separated and apart from your Lord as you are, having lost the hold and lost the bonding and seeking it again?

What could sustain you through the ravages of hell and the astral plane between embodiments? What could sustain your opportunity to live to love again except love itself?

Love is impersonal yet personal. As Saint Germain has said, God is an Impersonal Impersonality, an Impersonal Personality, a Personal Personality and a Personal Impersonality. When you have figured this out on the arms of the Maltese cross, beloved, come and tell me.[4] These are the definitions of God as Father and as Son and as Mother and as Holy Spirit.

O the light rays that pierce, that pierce the dawn of earth while coming from the Central Sun! Your eyes can scarcely open to behold such light and yet you know it at inner levels. You know its secret.

You have journeyed far, yet the call of the homing has been from the heart of earth. You have known you must come. And you who are here, one and all, share a common cup of love. You have desired to return to give, oh, so much more love than you allowed yourself to give or God to give through you in recent and ancient incarnations. You have regretted profoundly this withholding.

Now you see, now you know, now you understand that as you love all whom you meet, you will resolve and fulfill, dissolve and consign in and unto the flame all lesser manifestations. Love shall be unto you, if you claim her this night, the victory of your soul in this life.

There are others who have a dire need for truth, for they dwell not in the truth but in the lie. There are others who have a need for honor, for they have been dishonorable toward life. But the need of all here, and the desiring, is to be in that flame of love and to give it. This is what is the common note and the communality of all of you and of all upon earth who share the ascended masters' teachings.

For what is this teaching but the divine love of God, who has come to nurture your soul and answer her questions and give the divine doctrine?

The love you have received must beget great God-gratitude. Thus, in giving again and again, you, my beloved, shall reach for and pick that rose of light that comes from the heart of the Divine Mother.

In the bliss of God, I AM Clara Louise. Know that there is no true divine love without pain, for the pain is what true divine love flushes out. Fear not to touch upon and to experience ancient and recent pains —and let them pass, let them pass into the flame, into the river Ganges, into the hearts of saints and back to God.

Yes, beloved, let there no longer be the suppression, let there no longer be the placing of the wall around yourself to insulate yourself from pain. Pain approaches the edge of bliss then dissolves into it. This is the knowing of true love.

I wish you, with all of my heart and my prayers, the fulfilling of the mystery of love in this life. The mystery is elusive. It plays hide-and-seek with you.

The more love you carry, beloved, the more it shall cause the hatred to come out in others. You say, "How can this be true love?" True love is a purging fire. If you decide to carry it to such an intensity, you shall become the Refiner's fire.

Do not hold back your will from entering in to this experience, for many are the prisoners of their own hatreds of centuries. They cannot get away from them. They are in bondage. They cannot escape. It requires the surgery of love and the holding of that one until love does consume that wall of hatred.

If you fear to be bruised and beaten by those to whom you give love, then you are not yet ready to carry the Saviour's love. Begin with little loves, for they are seeds planted and they become beautiful unfolding flowers that grow and grow. You shall be strengthened in this process and you shall know little by little the gratitude that comes from those who could not have been saved unless you had embodied that flaming fire.

Many, many, beloved, are bound by the karma of love's perversions. Will you not be the representatives of angels and ascended masters of the third ray of love and of the Holy Spirit itself to speak to these ones, to minister to them?

Realize also that it is sometimes best that you remain anonymous, praying fervently and fasting even on behalf of those whom you know not, that they might receive that love and be liberated.

Contemplate, then, how great must be that love to liberate a single soul from the grips of death and hell. Truly the astral plane is a place where people are "brainwashed," as they say. Their minds are controlled to believe that that which is offered to them by fallen angels is in their best interest. To tear them from this and to give them the gift of beginning life over again under the true Divine Parents, this is the mighty, mighty work of love!

Know that it awaits you when you are ready.

And if you are just beginning this path, take up, then, love's own violet ray and flame and the purple fire and use it, beloved. Use it, I say, to purge yourself of love that is unreal and to fill yourself with love that is Real.

I am your friend on the path of love. If you call to me, I will give you a recounting of many, many incidents in my life in which I devised the means of self-discipline whereby I did conserve the sacred fire of love and therefore had the power, mighty indeed, to convey it to others who had nothing at all in the cups of their chakras.

Know this joy of being divine love in action to supply the love that only God can give and that you have stored in your cups. Give to those who are able to take of the cup of living love and not dash it. Retain and hold the balance for others who would only lose it, to their loss and yours.

Therefore be wise and let the All-Seeing Eye of God at the point of the brow become for you a point of single-minded, true discernment and discrimination in order that compassion may flow where compassion does compel.

I seal you in the ruby cross and the flame of the Ruby Buddha, who shall salute you in this conference.

Messenger's benediction:

I seal you in the light of Almighty God and his living Presence within you and I commend you now to keep this love in your heart, to go quietly to your place of rest and ask to be taken to the retreat of Luxor, the Ascension Temple of Serapis Bey, where the ascended lady master Clara Louise also serves with her twin flame, Amen Bey. May you be received there and instructed in the path of your life and what you shall accomplish because you love God's will and his wisdom and his promises more than your very life.

In the name of the Father, the Son, the Holy Spirit, and the Divine Mother, it is finished.

October 11, 1991
New Orleans, Louisiana

The ascended lady master Clara Louise was embodied as Clara Louise Kieninger (1883–1970). In 1961 Saint Germain anointed her as the first Mother of the Flame of the Keepers of the Flame Fraternity. For years she had devotedly served in the field of nursing, taking as her motto *Ich Dien* ("I serve"). Later, as a dedicated student of the ascended masters, Clara Louise kept a daily prayer vigil for the youth of the world, the incoming children and their parents and teachers. She would begin every morning at five and decree for two to four hours, and sometimes till noon. In her dictation given May 4, 1991, the ascended lady master Clara Louise told us: "I see so many among you for whom I did pray. . . and I would tell you that it is clear in the record that my prayers did make the difference in your entering the Path." In 1966, when the mantle of the office of Mother of the Flame was passed to the messenger Elizabeth Clare Prophet, Clara Louise became the Regent Mother of the Flame. She made her ascension at the age of 87 from Berkeley, California, on October 25, 1970. Her soul's devotion to God is also reflected in prior embodiments. In the days of Lemuria, she served in the central temple as a priestess at the altar of the Divine Mother, and at the time of Jesus she was embodied as the apostle James. From the ascended level, she continues to hold the office of Regent Mother of the Flame, nurturing the souls of all the world's children. She is the twin flame of the ascended master Amen Bey, who works closely with Serapis Bey in the Ascension Temple at Luxor, Egypt. Her keynote is "Calm As the Night."

(See *Ich Dien,* memoirs of Clara Louise Kieninger, edited and compiled by Elizabeth Clare Prophet, and *The Masters and Their Retreats,* pp. 56–61; both available at Store.SummitLighthouse.org.)

"A Soft Answer Turneth Away Wrath"

Excerpt from *Ich Dien,* the memoirs of Clara Louise Kieninger

On my return to the hospital, I was placed in a private pavilion as the head nurse. In the morning report, the night nurse reported a new patient had come in late at night for observation. He would not let the nurses do anything for him. He was an old bachelor and very unpleasant, she said.

In my rounds after the report, I knocked gently on this patient's door and opened it. He greeted me with "What do you want in here? Get out! I've never been bossed by a woman and I don't intend to start now."

I replied, "I came in to ask if you have a special wish for breakfast."

He replied: "You should know what a patient needs. Send it in, and do not come back." I sent it in to him.

Presently the bell rang and he asked that I come in. He was sitting up in bed with his breakfast tray on his lap. He said, "What do you call this? What kind of breakfast is this?"

I took the tray out and sent in another one. He said, "Now get out." . . .

In time he became softened and became a good patient. (We graduated in the fall of the year, and I invited him to the graduation.)

He called me into his room one day. He was sitting up in bed, and on his lap was a large tray of beautiful jewels. He said: "I want you to select whatever jewel or jewels you wish. They were my mother's, and I wish you to have some of them." I looked the tray over and selected a very simple gold bar pin.

He said, "I want you to take another pin, one of these diamond ones." I did not take any that he indicated, but finally selected an ivory rose and chain, which I wore later to all the early morning classes of Mother Mary. He insisted that I select some gorgeous piece, but to no avail.

In a few days he was dismissed from the hospital; and for my graduation he sent two dozen gorgeous American Beauty roses, a five-pound box of candy, and twenty-five dollars. Also, he came to the graduation, but left immediately after the service. I never saw him after that.

A soft answer turneth away wrath. In this particular patient, it brought about a complete change from a sour, bitter person to an understanding and friendly being.

CHAPTER 3

Lady Master Meta

THE MIRROR OF TRUTH

Be That Christ Truth and Prove and Reprove a World!

Now I come to you in the living flame of truth. Let truth, then, be in this hour the divine mirror. Thus, the mirror is before each one and I do mirror back to you your own state of consciousness. Let the mirror of truth reveal, then, the cause and effect of conditions in your world.

Be a scientist with me in this hour. You, as a devotee of Christ Truth, must unburden the ascended hosts as well as yourself of your troublesome state of mind wherein you do not know your Real Self or your unreal self and therefore cannot assess your progress on the Path or how others view you or why you find yourself in the circumstance in which you are.

The living flame of truth brings proof as well as reproof—yes, beloved, proof of causes set in motion and reproof as truth compels you to trace those causes as they become effects in the return current of karma. Thus, this mirror of truth becomes to you a crystal and the crystal does reveal many layers of consciousness.

You have come for knowledge but knowledge begins with self-knowledge. You who are or would be Keepers of the Flame of Life this day, keep the flame of self-knowledge: "I am my brother's keeper."

Keep the flame of truth, then, and know that truth shall pierce the veil and enable you to see the glory of the LORD.

What is this glory of the LORD?

It is the light manifestation of the I AM THAT I AM.

It is Christos.

It is the original Word with God.

It is Shakti.

Christ Jesus is the incarnation of that divine Shakti. Christ Jesus *is* that LORD. Thus, the cause is the I AM THAT I AM and the effect is Christos as Divine Mother—as the mirror of truth.

Do you question this truth, beloved?

Indeed the fire that does become the manifestation of the son or daughter of God is feminine, as it is in polarity with the fire of its origin. Thus, whether masculine or feminine avatar, the Christ is the eternal Divine Mother, is the eternal Word. The Christ is the power, the energy, the manifestation and the intensity of *light, light, light* that does purge the body of God in the earth when that body is truly ready for the purging.

Now behold the self in the mirror as I show you levels of your own spiritual pride, intellectual pride, human pride, the pride of the not-self, the unreal self. Be willing to look at this; for seeing this image allows you, then, to have the frame through which you will pass, by your dynamic decrees, the violet all-transmuting flame, the sacred fire.

Do not shun this yoga of mantra. Do not say, "I am above it." Except ye become as a little child and take the first steps of initiation, you will not enter in to the halls of truth.

Truth always reveals, as plain as plain for all to see, what is the substance that is real or unreal about each individual. When you espouse the flame of truth of our cohort of light, the beloved Pallas Athena, you shall know that truth, holy Truth, is the greatest comfort to all life.

Therefore the Comforter does come with the incarnation of Christ Truth in the Virgin. The Virgin is the archeia, the feminine complement of the archangel.[1] Thus, the holy Mary did descend as the archeia to give the protection of truth and comfort unto the Lord Jesus Christ.

Will you also raise him up?

Will you also know the glory, the Light/Christ manifestation, of that truth in you?

If you would, beloved, I tell you, you must know the guardian action of truth. You must see what is unreal and, in the very least, call to God to bind it and, in the very most, surrender it instantaneously into the flame of sacred fire. Those who are truly on the path of the resurrection will not compromise these facets day by day.

You who celebrate your birth from the beginning unto the ending this day and every day must know that the real rebirth in the Spirit of the living God is by Alpha, by Omega, by the admission that the unreal is not, and the Real is, by the confession of sin that is unreal, by the grace that does praise God for the revelation of Truth—that is Real.

You have been called to be mighty instruments of love. I call you to be instruments of truth. This does require not pride but courage, an immense courage that is emboldened by the Spirit of the LORD and by the sense of one's own humility before that power omnipotent.

The power of God shall never be transferred unto those who have not tasted the sweetness of Jesus Christ. The sweetness of truth may become the bitter fount for a time, changing all senses of the soul and the ability to know one's own spiritual environment.

This is a process of purging. Welcome it! Welcome the purging of the body and the mind. And do not become enangered when the voice of truth and the mirror of truth do reveal the underpinnings of a pride that shall shortly collapse of its own weight.

Better to pass your test and disassociate yourself from these ancient coils that go back to Mayan civilizations, to Atlantis, to civilizations on the continent of North America where the fallen ones did engage you on a path of mastery, not by the light magic of the hosts of the LORD but by the black magic of the fallen ones. Even in this area* and throughout the Caribbean there have been brought forth again such practices of enslavement of body and soul.

Those who manipulate power to their own ends use these modes. Those who allow themselves to be instruments of the power of God and to submit to its will and its commands need no such artifices.

*landed areas bordering on the Gulf of Mexico

They, beloved, have received the initiation of the all-power of God from the realms of light, from the realms of earth.

They, then, take dominion. But in taking dominion they must also recognize that the vigilance must increase; for those who embody power, even as those who embody true love, must surely give attention to the protection of that power and its manifestation in the physical body day by day.

You are as shorn lambs; therefore you have great need of the shepherd. Now let the Lamb of God be the shepherd in manifestation within you. Let the Christ descend into your temple! Let your Holy Christ Self be the reality of your manifestation!

And then guard well this dispensation and know that God shall not give unto you an increase in any of the divine attributes until you come to a reckoning of the forces of death and hell who move against the one who is in the earth crowned with that crown of the stars of the Cosmic Virgin.

Yes, understand, beloved, that God indeed has need of you in your truthful, fullest manifestation—you who see that the equation in the earth is one of the misuse of the power of God by those who are called the power elite, the misuse of the altar of God by those who have presented themselves in the priest class since Atlantis and Lemuria.

Let the divine equation be unto you that you understand that he who would defeat the forces of darkness on behalf of the children of light of a world must be ready for great surrender and a change of lifestyle and a twenty-four-hour attentiveness and vigilance in the protection of the community, even the sangha of the Buddha, even of the called-out ones of the Lord Christ.

Thus, God shall not bestow this initiation of the transfer of his all-power, though the fate and future of the entire world should depend upon it, unless the candidate to receive it is fully entrenched in the rigors of adeptship of the Great White Brotherhood.

Thus, beloved, we must test, we must try your spirit. We must know whether you are willing to put on that armour of God in increasing measure, whether you can remain vigilant, whether you can even remember the promises you have made to God and then keep them, even the words you have spoken in a whisper at the altar. All these are heard.

And councils of light who have been your mentors for aeons do consider whether you have come to that place of your divine manhood, your divine womanhood, where you can carry the scepter of power and yet withstand the challenge of those who come with their misused power, which they have stolen from the altar of God.

Why, then, do you suppose that you are powerless to heal, to raise the dead, to do anything about the circumstances in a darkening world?

It is because of this very equation, beloved. You might say that the evolutions of earth share this one singular collective karma: the abuse of power. Therefore have they been reduced to threescore and ten;[2] therefore have they been reduced to a minimum of energy so as not to allow those who have a record of the abuse of power to make a horrendous karma again and again.

See this equation, beloved, and see again in the mirror of self what folly it is to have pride in one's mind or intellect or supposed spiritual prowess, what folly it is to lean upon that power that is not truly the power of God, that mind, that Presence.

Against the backdrop, then, of the saints in white who surround you now, whose faces and presences you see in the mirror, take a measure of yourself if you can. Gauge your point on the Path and recognize that in your present state it is by the glory of the Lord and the grace of God that you even have opportunity to balance that karma of the abuse of power and step-by-step to enter anew the temple of Serapis Bey, the Dome of the Rock[3] of Hercules and Amazonia, or perhaps be in the presence of El Morya or Archangel Michael at their retreats at Darjeeling and Banff, to know again increment by increment the power of God.

My call to you, then, is to discipline yourself each day in the mastery of the increment of power that is yours, God-given. Let it be mastered in the chakras, in the spoken Word, in the third eye. And know that as you build solidly, that power does become a part of your identity and you become a part of it. Thus, as you build you will see that the forces of death and hell shall not prevail against you.

Do not take this discipline in isolation, as a lonely climber, but recognize that our Brotherhood has ordained the community of the Holy Spirit, the Mystery School of Lord Maitreya. Thus, by the reinforcement of many devotees at all steps and stages on the Path, both the weak and the strong in an unguarded moment are yet protected by the Circle of the One. Few solitary climbers make it on the Path, beloved.

Again, look into the mirror. I urge you to do so without hesitation, for it is a cosmic moment and dispensation that has not been given to you in this manner in your entire life and shall not be given to you again until you have fully used what has been revealed.

Thus, see and know, if you dare to look, how the forces of hell would move against you, how Archangel Michael does stand between you and them, how you need the hierarchy of the Great White Brotherhood (which consists of the sons and daughters of God, the archangels and cosmic beings and even the elementals).

See and know how God has conspired to put together this cosmic community of lightbearers and enlightened ones for mutual reinforcement in the days and hours of Armageddon, when hosts of darkness from distant spheres array themselves against the Woman clothed with the Sun, who does again and again bring forth the Divine Manchild as the Christ consciousness appearing in each and every one of you.

Pray diligently also for mothers with child who are bearing souls of light of greater attainment than their own. For parents come under the opposition of the fallen ones who attack the child, and these fallen ones have an attainment on the left-handed path commensurate with that of the incoming avatar on the right-handed path.

Therefore, beloved, the equation of the protection of fathers and mothers and families in the day of the appearing of the descent of souls of light should be in your heart and mind continually. For if the bearing of such a holy child should cause a mishap or an untimely removal from the screen of life of parents or sponsors, then, beloved, we do not send such a soul of light.

See how the earth is crying out for *light, light and light!* Whether it be embodied angels serving the good, elementals serving the good, people of God serving the God-good, they all, one and all, cry out for light and for deliverance! And some receive it and some do not. It is a karmic situation, but it is also a situation of non-karma: it is one of initiation.

Let the bold ones, then, be emboldened in the desire to receive light as an empowerment unto the giving to others of that light, unto the keeping of that light as guardians of the sacred fire!

O beloved, we have spoken in this wise for many years!

The giant leap that could take you beyond measures and measures of karma is a possibility. But if you would skip over the trends of your karma, which manifest as trends of your psychology, then you must have a self-discipline that is equal to that level of initiation to which you aspire. Only that self-discipline can win against the momentums of karma that pull you as an undertow of a great sea, a sea of darkness that moves in other directions than the direction of your Polestar.

How, then, is this to be accomplished?

How do you beat the fates of karma and psychology and arrive at the place where you are ready for that empowerment before it is too late for a world, a world that has been waiting for aeons for the glory of the Lord as the sunrise within you?

I will tell you, beloved. It is to affix your soul to the ascended master El Morya or to Saint Germain, principal Gurus who will carry you and teach you and accelerate you. Yes, there are some who will accept the word of one such as Morya and make swift strides. There are others who will move with Saint Germain. But Saint Germain does often send them back to El Morya to receive that foundational training.

Thus, beloved, El Morya awaits the call of the earnest soul who understands the meaning of daily and hourly obedience to precepts in order that that soul may not, then, repeat again and again and again the same mistakes, the same errors, the same disobediences.

If you can learn a lesson of God on this day and keep that lesson and move forward with that lesson sealed so that you shall never again compromise yourself on that lesson, you can know a path of true adeptship under the ascended masters, whose teachings are brought to you accurately by this messenger and by the ascended messenger, whose deliveries are amply recorded and printed.

Know, then, that the teaching is there, the sponsorship is there and the Great White Brotherhood does come close to you now. Behold, then, the glory of the saints as tens of thousands of these saints surround this place, envelop this city and show you how they are the presence of the swaddling garment of God in a protection of light in this moment that is almost smothering.

Yes, beloved, if you have a true desire for adeptship—not for spiritual pride but for the giving of the gift of self on behalf of those who have not the qualifications to attain that adeptship—then I tell you, heaven will not hold you back. There is no holding back of the one who is willing to move forward and who does recognize in this hour that chelas of self-mastery are the ones who must come forward if those prophecies that are coming upon the earth are to be stopped or mitigated.

A karma is descending. It is a grave karma, beloved. Of all those who speak positively, whether on the economy or the political events or of those situations that are transpiring in every nation, none can hide the darkness of the Dark Cycle. May you be a bright light within that cycle.

Now I show you upon the mirror that is before you the great darkness in the earth, the great darkness of the fallen ones. And I show you your Holy Christ Self and yourself one in that Christ, piercing that darkness, standing in the very center of it! And the light of that single Christ is the light that lightens an entire world.

The whole world can be filled with the glory of God! This is the calling of the legions of truth, of healing, of science, of the abundant life and of the two-edged sword of the fifth ray that cleaves asunder the Real from the unreal. Christ is Truth incarnate!

I, Meta, who come with my healing bands, salute you in that truth and I say, *be* that Christ Truth and prove and reprove a world!

As long as thou art in the world, thou art either the light of the world[4] or the darkness of the world. Choose this day! And cease your dallying in the gray area of self-conceit! For self-conceit is folly and it is death.

I, Meta, shall continue to impress upon you all Christ Truth until you dismiss me. Thus, I shall be with those of you who no longer desire the compromise of the human consciousness and you shall know what it means to be sponsored by a Mother of the fifth ray.

With Mary I come, with Pallas Athena, with the cosmic being Elohim Virginia. I come with a cosmos of the mind of the Cosmic Virgin and I am ready to assist you.

You *are* Christ Truth. I know it!

Do you know it, my beloved? [Audience replies, "Yes!"]

Oh then, I pray you, be wise, be wise, be wise!

Be it. Be it now.

October 12, 1991
New Orleans, Louisiana

The ascended lady master Meta serves on the fifth ray (green ray) of healing, science, and truth. She is the daughter of Sanat Kumara and Lady Master Venus, hierarchs of the planet Venus. On Atlantis, Meta tended the flame of healing in the healing temple, now focused in the etheric plane over New England. In a dictation given December 30, 1974, the ascended master Hilarion told us that Meta had volunteered to tarry with earth's evolutions. He said: "Meta, then, will occupy etheric levels of the atmosphere of the planet, serving in the various healing temples. Her assignment is to minister to the needs of children." He said that Meta would be at hand to help mothers and fathers with problems with their children and to heal the minds of children from harmful influences. She is assisted by priestesses of the sacred fire who have tended the flame of healing for thousands of years and who will come to the bedside of children in answer to our call. Meta works with all the healing masters and the angelic hosts. She carries in her consciousness the immaculate concept, the pure and perfect crystal design, for every child on earth and those coming into embodiment. Hilarion recommended that we appeal to Meta to transfer the crystal matrix for our children. He said: "You can call for the healing thoughtform and the crystal of the immaculate concept to be anchored in their etheric bodies, even now in this very moment. Each day call upon Meta and you will see how your children will preserve the crystal clarity of the consciousness of God that they had upon entering the world scene."

CHAPTER 4

Lady Master Nada

SO GREAT A LOVE

Self-Givingness unto God: The Key to Empowerment

How, then, shall you endure so great a salvation?[1]

How shall you endure so great a love?

Only love will allow you to fulfill this call of beloved Meta. Love so supplies you with the holiness of a divine completion that you are able, then, to remember hour upon hour the joyous discipline of love.

O how ready is our God! O such love! May you feel now the presence of the archangel Chamuel and of Charity, of myself and of the Elohim of love, Heros and Amora. Feel now the love of the Holy Spirit. Feel the love of Paul the Venetian. Feel that love, O my beloved, and see if once having touched and been touched by this love you can even bear to be without it for a moment.

This love of the love of God inspires meditation upon the One, the dissolving of self into the Greater Self until the Greater Self does displace the lesser self and appear as thine own True Self.

Is this not love's own alchemy—you so desiring to enter into the love of God and to have the love of God contain thee?

Yes, for love and love alone men and nations will sacrifice. They will bend the knee. They will come upon the Holy of Holies.

They will know an inner walk with God that is the cosmic wheel turning as the great wagon wheel of life that crosses the prairies, the continents and even becomes the wheel of an Elijah's chariot.

Yes, the wheel of love propels you onward in this service. Service unto life is a self-givingness. O that givingness unto God! O that givingness unto God! This is the key to empowerment.

Yes, you will meet those of the East. They are many who have worked for the *siddhis,* the *vibhutis.*[2] They have worked for them, beloved. They have attained them. But they have no moral fiber, no character in Christ. They are not soon to be the Buddha, not even having been accepted on the path of the bodhisattva. Yet they come to the West plying their wares, and the silly ones flock after them, are traduced and seduced by them.

Yes, beloved, beware the false teachers out of the East. Go not there but go to the kingdom of God that is within you.[3] Go to divine love: for the cup of divine love is all healing power, is all the power of alchemy for the transformation of a world by love.

What of the selflessness?

I have described it. It is the Greater Self appearing. Desire this birth! Desire this birth. Desire this cosmic conception of the Higher Self within you. Desire to see the sugar cube of self dissolved and to allow the fear, the ultimate fear of the loss of self, to be endured. For suddenly, in a moment, true divine love descending shall swallow up that not-self, that fear, and true divine love shall unveil the one who is thy true divine nature.

Give birth to this, beloved! Give birth to this. Then thou shalt know new pinions that shall carry thee into new realms of light.

I AM Nada. My love, so intense for all, has enabled me to accept and fulfill my responsibilities as a member of the Karmic Board and as the Lord of the sixth ray. It is the grace of Jesus Christ. It is the grace of Lord Maitreya. It is the grace of Gautama Buddha. It is the grace of Sanat Kumara.

I am one with the ruby ray masters and the Dhyani Buddhas. Thus, my greatest sense of self is "God is Love where I am." Love where I am can and does and shall never fail to meet all needs of the hour for all who call upon me and for all to whom I have pledged my responsibility for love's perfect bloom.

Let the soul blossom freely! Let the soul fear not to unfold her petals! Let the soul fear not to enter God, to be God! Let the soul fear not the entering of God unto herself. Let the soul fear not the divine Lover, to be wooed and to be loved, to be assimilated, to be reborn again.

Thou shalt have many lifetimes within this life if thou dost choose the path of love's hurrying. If anyone says to you, "What is your hurry?" simply say: "I am hurrying to keep up with Nada, with my divine Lover, with the One who calls me. And as I run to answer the call I must keep running, for my divine Lover is the God who is the Spirit of the LORD, who does ever engage in the process of self-transcendence and therefore I must become love's newness day by day."

Yes, beloved, you can indeed fulfill all things when you get rid of the sense of self and enter into the Real Self. Fear not. You shall still have this body and this mind, but they shall be renovated by such bands as those of Saint Francis.[4] They shall be rebuilt and remade.

Yes, beloved, a newness of life can come upon you! Understand there is a fear in the sinews and in the bones and in the organs to let go of the sense of self. It involves the fear of death itself, and yet death and resurrection is the theme of the path of the Christed ones.

Why wait till the end of life to die all at once, when in dying a little each day,[5] you can put on a portion of the deathless Self each day? Thus, when the hour of change does ultimately come, you are already the deathless Self clothed in the deathless solar body.[6]

It is a shame to wait, beloved ones, for the fire of the resurrection is intense. Its very purpose necessitates an accelerated fire, for it accelerates the light atoms of your being and takes you to the point of light from which you descended so very, very long ago.

This earth is a scene of the forgetfulness of love. People long to taste the love of God again, but they have forgotten the taste and will not know it until they taste it again. Thus, they accept many harmful substances as a substitute. But once the elixir is quaffed in this life, you should never again know the forgetfulness of the absence of love —which absence is caused by yourself.

We speak in terms of a divine mysticism, but the true mystics are the only truly practical people. They are those who can live in this earth, make their mark, be effective and themselves overcome the traducing, seducing ones by a spirit of reality that is akin to the spirit of truth and the piercing white of the honor flame.

Seek the honor of God, then, and know that love will fulfill the whole law of adeptship in you if only you will fulfill love's law. It is a simple message, beloved, but it is an ancient call that has echoed down the channels of the centuries.

You are, as it were, at the bottom of a channel of light that goes to the Central Sun and you hear echoing down its chamber the call of divine love. It seems so very far away, yet it is transmitted through your own heartbeat.

You can ascend the spiral. Therefore, call daily for the transmutation of the gravity of karma. And I mean this word in both senses, for karma is both grave and heavy and, when untransmuted, it shall take you to your grave, unfulfilled by light. The gravity of earth signifies the weight of world karma.

Be lightless and filled with light! Be emptied of light misused and filled with light correctly used.

I speak for the chohans, the lords of the seven rays, today, who invite you anew to call to be taken to their universities of the Spirit[7] that you might be God-taught and be of ultimate usefulness unto God in this window of opportunity that this decade presents.

I AM Nada of the living flame of love.

Let your love also be a living love flame!

October 12, 1991
New Orleans, Louisiana

The ascended lady master Nada is the chohan of the sixth ray (purple and gold ray) of ministration and service. She is also a member of the Karmic Board, on which she serves as the representative of the third ray (pink ray) of divine love. From Nada we learn the practical application of love and the path of personal Christhood through ministration and service to life. On Atlantis Nada worked in the healing arts and served as a priestess in the Temple of Love. The etheric counterpart of this temple, which is designed after the pattern of a rose, is centered above New Bedford, Massachusetts. She was also embodied as a lawyer on Atlantis, where she championed the cause of divine justice for the downtrodden and oppressed. In her final incarnation 2,700 years ago, Nada was the youngest of a large family of exceptionally gifted children. She was tutored by Charity, Archeia of the Third Ray, in how to expand the threefold flame of love in her heart for the quickening of the chakras of her talented brothers and sisters. She chose to forgo pursuing her own career in that embodiment and instead kept the flame in deep meditation and prayer for her brothers and sisters in their various fields of endeavor. In her dictation on August 28, 1982, Nada spoke of that lifetime: "I can assure you that at the conclusion of my incarnation when I saw the victory of each one of my brothers and sisters, the fullness of my joy was in a heart of love expanded. . . . It seemed to the world, and perhaps even to my own, that I had not accomplished much. But I took my leave into the higher octaves thoroughly understanding the meaning of the self-mastery of the pink flame. Thus it was from the point of the third ray that I entered into the heart of Christ and saw the application on the sixth ray as ministration and service." The ascended lady master Nada assists ministers, missionaries, teachers, healers, psychologists, counsellors at law and public servants—all who are involved in serving the needs of others. She teaches at the retreat of Jesus in the etheric octave over Saudi Arabia, where she instructs on the God-mastery of the emotions and the quieting of inordinate desire. Nada is an initiate and master of the path of the ruby ray. She is very much involved with the initiation and sponsorship of twin flames and the Aquarian-age family. She also ministers to the world's children with legions of angels who personally tend to the needs of the youth.

(See *Lords of the Seven Rays,* Book One, pp. 203–18; Book Two, pp. 461–90; and *The Masters and Their Retreats,* pp. 238–41.)

CHAPTER 5

Bodhisattva Kuan Yin

"FORGIVE AND BE FORGIVEN"

Enter the Circle of the One

Without the mercy and forgiveness of God there can be no rejoicing in the heart of the daughter of Zion. Mercy, therefore, is the foundation of the return; forgiveness, therefore, is the foundation of the return—of the assimilation of thy soul by the living Christ and the Lord Buddha.

I AM Kuan Yin, the open door unto the Amitabha Buddha. I am the opening of the way unto the mercy of God, which you must first give to God if you would receive it from him.

Give mercy unto God and forgive God of all those things that you have blamed him for. You may not know that you have blamed God but in subconscious, unconscious levels of being, many, in fact the majority, do hold against God the circumstances of the karmic law of retribution that does affect them. Therefore there is an anger against God and a nonforgiving of God.

If you would be forgiven, beloved, you must first recognize that it is you who have transgressed against God. Call upon the law of forgiveness. See yourself drenched in a holy unguent of purple fire, in a balm of violet ray. See yourself receiving that mercy in proportion as you give it, for it is the Law that you will reap mercy only as you sow mercy.

Then know that your heart shall truly rejoice, even as your heart rejoices when you know you have done well and served with a pure heart and therefore you can accept yourself and God can accept you.

Know, then, that the days and lifetimes of your impurity or uncleanness and of the sensing thereof recall a karma that has rested upon you and endured, for the karmic law has exacted it.

But in this day and in this hour you come under the new dispensation, when by the violet flame that is mercy's flame—which is always released when you give my mantras[1]—the opportunity does open unto lightbearers of the world for the acceleration of the balancing of karma such has not been seen in many, many ages.

Such an opportunity to be restored to wholeness, to set one's feet upon the path of life again! Oh yes, beloved, the rejoicing to know that God has accepted thee as his son, his daughter, and that the curse of the name "sinner" is broken and that you can return to God by love through mercy even as you give mercy to others.

It has been spoken before but we have come to offer you a trilogy, a triptych if you wish, a panorama of truth and love and mercy, that you might understand that these are truly the ingredients of the rejoicing of a mother's heart in seeing the image of Christ once again upon your face and the face of your soul.

I, too, represent the Karmic Board and I served as the Lord of the seventh ray before Saint Germain took that office. I am the bodhisattva who has tarried long with the evolutions of earth. I minister unto all but I am here specifically to assist the original lightbearers of God to attain to that level of Christhood which they once knew. This I do in order that they might in turn *be* the God or Goddess of Mercy on planet Earth for children who have yet to reach that level.

I place my Electronic Presence this day over one million souls who have known the point of Christhood with Jesus Christ in ancient days of Atlantis and in ancient days of India.[2] So they have come again and many have exchanged their robes for the robes of this world.

And this brings me full circle to the subject of the robe of the pride of the intellect and its narrow band of attainment. Yes, beloved, these individuals have exchanged the robe of Christhood in the mind of

God for the robe of pride—pride in the path of that human will, that human personality and that human mind.

Therefore, I say to all: call for the divine exchange and let it take place day by day smoothly, old garments for new—imperfect truth, imperfect love, imperfect mercy for the perfect all three, the perfection of all three. Yes, tender ones, loving ones who seek to be as we are, we are with you.

Now mercy's flame and cup is offered to one million souls. Some receive it, some do not. I regularly assign my angels to this task. Those angels whose cups are rejected are themselves dejected, for they are burdened when souls who have had so great a light have now so great a pride that they do not understand how great is their need for mercy and for the forgiveness of God.

I AM Kuan Yin and, as I sit on the Karmic Board, I am involved in all legal matters. Call to me for mercy in mitigating the judgments of this world and even the judgments of the Karmic Board. Call to beloved Portia, twin flame of Saint Germain, for divine justice and then to me for mercy's flame to be added to that justice.

Yes, many matters are before the courts of the world today and many individuals will not receive the true and just verdict or sentencing. Many are abused, mistreated, yes, beloved.

Know, then, that your continual calls for the seven archangels to overshadow the judges, the magistrates and the rulers of the people in this world are indeed in order. Call to the archangels, then, whenever you must face those who hold the reins of power, for the advice is still well-taken: "Render unto Caesar the things that are Caesar's and unto God the things that are God's."[3]

The surest path to divine justice and divine mercy is the violet flame. The surest path to soul liberation and the balancing of karma is the violet flame! The surest path to adeptship in the flame of Christ Truth is the violet flame! The surest path to the expansion of the heart is the love meditation in mercy's ray.

So forgive and be forgiven.

So extend true justice and receive true justice in kind.

I AM Kuan Yin and I am touching the seat-of-the-soul chakra of each one. It is with an awakening love, as the Divine Mother should come upon you to gently fold back the covers that you might awaken to the morning light of mercy's flame and feel the healing power of God's mercy.

How tenderly do the angels of mercy care for you now! Call to them in the coming days that you might know such a profound sense of inner resolution in all conditions in your life.

Mercy is as mercy does. It is not a passive flame but wholly active. Be active in forgiving and receiving forgiveness. In the giving and receiving of forgiveness you are impelled to action for the very gratitude of such a mercy as can absolve all things, yes, all things, beloved.

There is no sin that is outside of the pale of mercy's flame. All things can be forgiven. Some sins that are greater require greater effort, compensation and transmutation, but in the end forgiveness can be given but only unto those who forgive in like measure unto a universe, as the universe does measure out mercy unto them.

With a grateful heart, therefore, go forth. For without mercy, you cannot be Christ Truth in action. Without mercy, love shall be compromised. O beloved, this is the nectar of the Buddhas! It is mercy's elixir.

If you have hardness of heart, choose your violet-flame decrees and my mantras and engage in perpetual mantra-giving as the heart and the mind have impressed upon them the mantra and as the mantra begins to sing in you even as you sing in it.

Mantras of mercy will wear down layers upon layers upon layers of nonmercy in your tree of life as nothing else will. See how by mercy's flame you shall be delivered of the karma—the group karma of a world that has abused God's power, beloved.

Remember, I did it. So can you.

I leave you with a cup of mercy's flame in your hand. May you drink a sip daily and a sip again and again. It is potent, beloved, a potent potion, as they say. Take it, then.

And all who are my children, now bringing me violets of mercy, so I say to you, dear elementals and sweet children of Christ Jesus and the Buddha Gautama, be blessed by your own merciful hearts and rise now to the retreat of Eriel of the Light that you might rejoice in elementals' receiving of mercy's flame through the calls of Keepers of the Flame.[4]

Know this law, beloved: When your heart shall be filled with the fullness of God's mercy, then and only then shall you know yourself in the Circle of the One, in the *law* of the circle, in the *protection* of the circle, in the *perfection* of the circle.

So I AM Kuan Shih Yin. My ministry is unto all life. Come and join me. I would teach you of the ministry of the brothers and sisters of mercy.

October 12, 1991
New Orleans, Louisiana

The bodhisattva Kuan Yin is known as the Goddess of Mercy because she ensouls the God qualities of mercy, compassion, and forgiveness. She serves on the Karmic Board as the representative of the seventh ray (violet ray). She also held the office of Chohan of the Seventh Ray for two thousand years until Saint Germain assumed that office in the late 1700s. Kuan Yin ascended thousands of years ago and has taken the vow of the bodhisattva to serve planet Earth until all her evolutions are free. From her etheric retreat, the Temple of Mercy, over Beijing, China, she ministers to the souls of humanity, teaching them to balance their karma and fulfill their divine plan through loving service to life and application of the violet flame. In Chinese Buddhism, Kuan Yin is seen as the feminine form of the Indian and Tibetan Avalokiteśvara—an emanation of the Dhyani Buddha Amitabha. Legends recount that Avalokiteśvara was "born" from a ray of white light that emitted from Amitabha's right eye. Kuan Yin is also appealed to as the "bestower of children" and patroness of fishermen. Mother Mary once told us: "The blessed Kuan Yin has become known as the Saviouress out of the East performing the selfsame and identical function as my own, yet each of us bringing to this office of Mother our past attainment and experience, which is different by our very service on differing rays."

In a dictation given on Mother's Day, May 8, 1988, Kuan Yin said: "I ask you to prove me, to make your demands upon me and to command my light and to keep on so doing until you should sense you have reached the limitations of my office. For I tell you, beloved, there is no thing of the will of God that I will not alchemically precipitate if you are able to bear it, if you are able to hold the harmony for it, and if you will seek the internal integration of the soul in the seventh-ray chakra with the fiery heart of the living Christ Bodhisattva."

(See *Kuan Yin Opens the Door to the Golden Age,* 1982 *Pearls of Wisdom,* vol. 25, Book I, pp. *1–80,* Book II, pp. *81–140;* and "The Compassionate Saviouress," in *Kuan Yin's Crystal Rosary* booklet, pp. 1–11.)

CHAPTER 6

The Buddha of the Ruby Ray

I PLANT THE SEED OF THE RUBY RAY IN THE CHALICE PREPARED

To Receive the Ancient Instruction of the Mentors of Shamballa on the Building of the Chalice, Come to Maitreya's Mystery School!

I AM indeed the Buddha of the Ruby Ray. I come quickly, and the Light of the Central Sun is with me. It is my reward and it can be thine also.

God in thee is the seed of the Buddha and I would plant the seed of the Buddha in the chalice prepared. The preparation of the chalice is an assignment that was given to you in ages past as you were instructed by your mentors from Shamballa, mentors who went forth across the earth to contact the original souls who had journeyed here with the Ancient of Days.[1]

Thus, they gave to you the careful instruction for the preparation of the chalice, of the four lower bodies, of the soul, the heart, the mind, the chakras. This memory is held by you vividly. Just beneath your conscious awareness, your soul retains the memory.

Some have served with great diligence to be prepared for the hour of my promised coming. This is my first coming, beloved. It is my coming whereby I may reward with my reward of light those who have been faithful to the instruction and to their promise to keep it.

Now then, some are prepared. Some have drifted into forgetfulness and untidiness in the preparation of the chalice.

Crystal upon crystal, you build around the frame and body that you wear an incorporeal light chalice. It is the vessel of the soul. Those who build it are truly the builders who have been so called from the ancient days, even those among you who did assist in the building of the original Shamballa on the island in the Gobi Sea.

Thus, building is your natural endowment, for you have built the stupas of the Buddha, the grand cathedrals of Europe and the ancient temples of Atlantis and even Lemuria. Building a citadel of light, then, is your joy, building around the secret chamber of the heart, even the temple for the coming of the Lord Gautama Buddha.

This building not made with hands[2] has been constructed by your souls. Some buildings are simple, some more elaborate, some well-nigh completion, some with barely the foundation begun.

Thus, beloved, in your temple you have laid a cornerstone and that cornerstone is the Rock of the living Christ, whom you adore and who is that point of the magnet of being, the central stone, the cornerstone remembered in masonry as the stone of Christ-potential that must come to full manifestation.

As you continue to build, as you have had reawakened in you this day the necessity for this building of the chalice, so I shall come again on occasion down the decades to reward you with that seed planted in the special place upon the altar within your building.

Now then, I speak to you of how you shall accomplish this task, for it is apropos to the subjects brought to your attention during this conference by the ascended masters.

Take particular note that Archangel Michael called you to seek adeptship[3] on the occasion of the thirty-third anniversary of The Summit Lighthouse, its founding in Philadelphia. Take note that Meta has called you to a path and that you have been reminded to balance the karma of the misuse of God's power that you might receive power once again—the power of Alpha, the power of Omega, of heaven and of earth.[4]

Note, then, the caution that you must take in guarding the action of protection, in keeping the discipline of love, of entering into the light and choosing mercy as the means of the opening of the flower of the heart.

Blessed ones, to teach you how to come forward and to hold the light and to protect it and to retain your God-harmony, to teach you to give the calls for the binding of the hosts of darkness, the hordes of death and hell and those who remain in physical embodiment and on the astral plane as practitioners of the black arts, which practices they have followed for many centuries—I am called to Summit University.

Blessed ones, those who arrive at the gate of power shall be assailed by the fallen ones. And if they do not have considerable self-mastery, the fallen ones shall move together as one host of Darkness to cut down that one who dares to rise in the power of God, the wisdom of God, and the love of God in the purity of the balance of the Divine Mother on planet Earth.

Thus, I tell you each one, it is simply not possible to impart the secrets of Maitreya's Mystery School in an open conference in a hotel in *any* city. Such impartations heart to heart from the masters through the messenger to you must be given in a setting that is sealed and protected and sponsored.

Therefore, those of you who earnestly seek this transfer of light and to master the art of protection and to be invited to be with Archangel Michael and his legions, going forth each night in full armour to assist in these battles,[5] must come to the Inner Retreat. And I bid you come quickly, while the opportunity is at hand in this decade to learn so many of the mysteries of God and the techniques of dealing with conditions such as those that exist on planet Earth.

Come, then, to Maitreya's Mystery School for winter quarter 1992. Understand the meaning of this opportunity:

It is the desire of the ascended masters and the messenger to give you that self-confidence, that independence, and that individuality in God so that wherever you find yourself on earth, on the inner planes, and beyond this life, you shall retain the conscious knowledge of how to deal with all circumstances that may come upon you by karma, by initiation or by the direct confrontation of fallen angels. To impart this heart to heart is our desire.

I speak on behalf of Padma Sambhava (the sponsoring Guru of your messenger), of Jesus Christ, Lord Maitreya, Gautama Buddha, and Sanat Kumara. I speak on behalf, beloved, of the Five Dhyani Buddhas. Yes, beloved, we would transmit to you not only knowledge but the means of self-discipline, for surely we desire to transfer that power of God, and quickly, so that you might aid and assist the many.

The time has come for you to understand that all chelas are not equal and those who consider themselves the first may find themselves the last. But to be last or first signifies that you are called and chosen. Better to be last, then, than the one beyond the last who did not enter in.

Understand, therefore, that at Maitreya's Mystery School every chela as bodhisattva on the Path is dealt with individually and personally according to the record of the Keeper of the Scrolls, the record of the Book of Life[6] and the individual karmic book of life.

Yes, beloved, you may not grade yourself or measure yourself, but you must come to Summit University knowing that the ascended masters will deal with you individually according to your strength, your weakness, your attainment or lack of it, according to the honor flame you have kept with the Brotherhood, according to your faithfulness, your reliability and trustworthiness.

There is a need upon earth in the nations and the cities, across the margents and even across the planes of consciousness for pillars of fire to stand and still stand in all octaves to hold the balance and preserve the opportunity for a golden age-to-be: a golden age to be in these lower octaves and not alone at etheric levels.

Therefore, beloved, the age of true empowerment has come. If you are not ready, be willing to make yourself ready. Be willing to pursue for whatever time or extended time may be required of you that you might receive the full prize.

Thus, I have in fact come to announce to you the opening of the doors by Maitreya to the paths and initiations of the bodhisattvas, the very ones who abide with Maitreya in higher levels of the etheric octave, the unascended ones who look to the day of their return when the Darkness of earth does recede and the Light does dawn again.

All those who keep the flame in this hour of earth's great travail shall know a strength and an attainment for having stood fast.

Therefore count your opportunity as wondrous, as mighty and as holy in the Lord to be in the earth, to have access to the adepts, to receive that transfer of light and knowledge.

I tell you frankly, as it is known by the hierarchy today, beloved, were it not for this messenger clothed upon with the mantle of Lord Gautama, you would not receive direct instruction and initiation. And it would be more arduous for you to make your way to the etheric retreats without the sponsorship of that mantle holding the balance for you. Recently El Morya so gave this instruction to the staff of the messenger.

When the messenger did come before the Lords of Karma to receive the assignment of this life, she was given the opportunity of two paths: the one, to become a Guru in the Himalayas with a small band of disciples, unknown to the world and therefore far from the reaches of the arrows and slings of outrageous fortune, far from the attack of the fallen ones, the attack of the press and the agencies of government and the people who are angry against the light. And the other, to come forward and be in the public eye and therefore be vulnerable to every level of opposition from all planes.

She was shown how only a few disciples would benefit from her mission in the serenity of the Himalayan fastnesses. She was shown the many thousands of souls who would receive benefit, who would have the opportunity for the ascension and who could be sponsored through her mantle should she take the course that would place her, then, at the forefront of the battle and subject to all onslaughts coming out of Church and State.

You can see the path that she has chosen. Therefore El Morya did state that more than 95 percent of those who have found this path and who are ascending to God would not have had this teaching had she not made this decision.

But as a result of this decision, beloved, those who do receive the light and the teaching must understand that the door which has been opened through the messenger is a door that will not be shut. And all who have betrayed the Christ and the Buddha in all past ages, who have fooled the people throughout the centuries and fed them the husks while keeping from them the true bread and the wine—they, then, because of their betrayal against God, are in the depths of their beings angry against the liberating power of the Word that you have received.

Thus, as a recompense for your chelaship unto the ascended masters and unto the mantle of the Guru that is borne by the messenger, remember to keep the flame of protection of the office and of the body and the mind and the heart and the service and the mission of the messenger that you and millions of others may be liberated by the work of the Divine Mother through her and through you.

Many of you have made stunning progress on the Path and are stars in the sea of maya. Your light shines to the heavens. And you have made this progress, some in decades and some in less, through your studies of the teachings published under The Summit Lighthouse.

Know, then, how you have traversed lifetimes of karma and how those who have gone before you who have passed from the screen of life through this activity have either entered octaves of light or made their ascension.

Truly the Lighthouse is not only the beacon light in a darkened world but also the open door for heaven to step through and commune directly with you. And it is the goal, beloved, that the messenger as the go-between should eventually not be needed but that you should have —through the bonding of your soul to the living Christ in you—that direct and perpetual contact.

This can come, beloved, only when you are able to seal the rents in the garment, to heal them and to see them mended by angels. For the accuracy in communication must be exact else even at a very high level of attainment you could still fall by the deceptions of the fallen ones.

Therefore, beloved, understand that you, too, are moving up the spiral, the thirty-three-tiered spiral, to your own personal victory. This is an hour to hold fast, to stand fast, and to know yourselves as a guardian action of light to protect the message and the messenger, the teaching and the Path.

The calls that must be made for this victory require a momentum, and the gaining of this momentum in the power of the spoken Word, beloved, is what coming to the Inner Retreat is all about.

To know the mysteries, to know the Path and the teaching, to know the meaning of absolute Darkness and absolute Light, of absolute Evil and absolute Good, to know the meaning of the two-edged sword, of the All-Seeing Eye of God and the sacred fire raised up, you must receive the teachings on these subjects that I must impart to you one by one.

Thus, beloved, cherish and value this opportunity, for it is an opportunity to balance much karma under the protection of the ascended masters. And the ascended masters receive dispensations and continue to receive them because of the work of the messenger and the staff and the Keepers of the Flame and the chelas of the will of God and all who apply themselves to this path who may not even be affiliated with this organization.

Know, then, beloved, that your assignment is with you, the protection of God is with you, and the light of the messenger is with you. Remember the words of Jesus to his disciples: "Work while you have the light, for the night cometh when no man shall work."[7]

The light is the incarnation of the Word. The light is your Holy Christ Self. The light is also the presence of the Brotherhood that can descend through the messenger because it is a dispensation that is sealed and ordained of God.

The great rejoicing of the messenger and yourselves on the occasion of the thirty-third anniversary of The Summit Lighthouse was that a new spiral of the thirty-three was commenced again. And though not all things were accomplished in the first thirty-three years that could have been, there is surely a tremendous progress and accomplishment that has been won. Now, then, that the dispensation is renewed, what opportunity lies before you!

Thus, Archangel Michael did explain that to take full advantage of that opportunity in these thirty-three years that do lie before you, you must seek adeptship and self-mastery in the physical octave and in the physical body—in the mind and in the heart. As you set yourself to do this, beloved, the Lord will lean upon you even as you lean upon the staff of the Lord and the staff of the messenger.

Now angels whom you have not met so recently are come, angels of the ruby ray, and they select from among you those who have elected to follow the ancient instruction of the mentors of Shamballa to build the chalice prepared.

Now I, the Buddha of the Ruby Ray, do place the seed in the chalice prepared. Where the chalice is not sufficiently prepared, I withhold the seed. It has the stamp of the code of your life, of your causal body upon it. I shall hold these seeds as you now accelerate, with all tools given to you, to have the chalice prepared.

This is the moment, then, when the angel of the ruby ray does place that seed in the chalices of those who are ready. [50-second pause]

It is done. Those of you who have received it have received it in the chakra of its appointing. There it is sealed. There it does begin a cycle of gestation and these cycles shall be determined by your own life cycles and momentum, measured by your application and your continuing building.

O be quickened now as the Keeper of the Scrolls does hand to you that scroll on which is written the meticulous instruction originally given to you by the mentor of Shamballa on the building of the chalice.

[7-second pause]

I place my Electronic Presence over those who are able to receive me without discomfort. It shall remain twenty-four hours and longer according to your ability to be and to remain congruent with me.

Some of you have a momentum in giving "The LORD's Ritual of Exorcism," an action of the ruby ray, or "The LORD's Judgment by the Ruby Ray." Thus, you have developed a certain co-measurement and coequation with the ruby ray. Some of you may receive a stronger or a less-concentrated manifestation of myself according to your aura.

Take note this day that what is marked clearly is an individual path unique to each chela, unique to the level of karma and the level of bonding to the Guru whom you can see and therefore to the Guru whom you see not. Seek early the bonding of the heart in a sweet love tie to your messenger, who loves you from the most profound depths of her being to the most profound depths of your own.

Fear not the bonding of brother and sister in community through the Holy Spirit. Fear not this oneness. For love is the foundation and the fount of all power of God.

Therefore I say, take up the sword of the ruby ray! Slice through fear and doubt! Cast them out! Let them be removed. And sing the song of the New Day.

O thou seed of God, thou who dost contain the allness of this individualization of the God flame in the smallness of self, even as the grain of mustard seed does bring forth the giant tree, so let the tree of life prosper. Let the seed restored, then, be for the pattern of identity to manifest here below as Above.

I AM the Buddha of the Ruby Ray.

I pronounce my inner name. [15-second pause]

I have come. I have placed the seed in the chalice prepared and I return to other dimensions yet remain close at hand.

Reach out your hand now and receive my own, beloved. Feel my touch. Feel my compassion. Feel my comfort. Welcome my chastening rod. Know this: I shall not leave you where I have found you.

Thus, come. Come up higher! Let us climb the mountain together. Let us climb the highest mountain.

October 12, 1991
New Orleans, Louisiana

The Buddha of the Ruby Ray was sent long ago by Sanat Kumara and Gautama Buddha to abide in the secret chamber of God in the heart of the earth. In his dictation on July 3, 1988, the Buddha of the Ruby Ray spoke of his acceptance of this assignment: "Think back now upon the day when you did see me, as from Shamballa I went forth. . . . All did watch as staff in hand, ruby ray focus about my neck, I did enter a cave and I did begin to walk and I did walk to the center of the earth. . . . I was told in that hour and all heard it, 'You shall not come forth until there be those on the surface of the earth who can hold the balance for the attainment that shall be thine own.' So, beloved, you might say that I have been confined to hold the nucleus of a planet at the mercy of such as yourselves until you should arrive at the place of a similar love for the ruby ray." In that dictation, the Buddha of the Ruby Ray gave us a gift of a droplet of ruby ray, which he said could be retained by us only if we kept the flame of internal love and harmony. He said: "I come to reinforce buddhic presence in your heart and leave indeed a replica, in outline only, of my form that you may fill in as you become the Buddha and see me mirrored in self. For I desire to live on the surface of earth in the hearts of true devotees of the Buddha. It is my prayer that you will accord me this to make my wish come true." During the 1989 Harvest class, Cuzco announced that the Buddha of the Ruby Ray, in answer to the call of the Keepers of the Flame, had literally walked step by step from the center of the earth to be present in our community and to assist us in dealing with the negative forces at hand. Let us remember to give the mantra dictated by Lanello, February 26, 1986:

Let the ruby ray and the ruby ray angels and the Buddha of the Ruby Ray dissolve now all darkness pitted against the Church Universal and Triumphant!

(See the Buddha of the Ruby Ray, 1986 *Pearls of Wisdom,* vol. 29, no. 73, and 1988 *Pearls of Wisdom,* vol. 31, no. 69.)

CHAPTER 7

Ernon, Rai of Suern

LESSONS LEARNED

The Remnant of the House of Israel

Good evening, sons and daughters of God. It gives me good pleasure to address you after long centuries of being apart from this evolution. Now from the ascended state I speak to you out of the love fount of my heart.

I come, then, to tell you of the lessons learned—lessons that I have learned, lessons that the Suernis have learned, and lessons that you have learned.

Of the two million who came with the Lord Christ to the land of Suern, who were his adherents and had considerable development of the Christ embodied within them, the one million who eventually ascended were in a state of higher love and higher grace. It was by their love for the living Christ and the Source whence he had come that they ascended from that land.

The one million who did not ascend, though they had Christ-attainment, did not have the sufficiency of love to sustain that level of devotion that would allow them to merit the ascension. And so the residue of their karma held them back and eventually did overtake them as they did multiply the negative momentums and did gradually let go of the positive momentums. Thus, increment by increment the sacred fire fell, almost unnoticeably yet precipitously.

These individuals have come to be known as the lost sheep of the house of Israel.[1] Thus, when Jesus came two thousand years ago he declared, "I am not sent but unto the lost sheep of the house of Israel."[2]

He came to call to repentance and to call to the path of the Divine Mother these remaining one million souls. Most of them are still embodied upon earth today, often in positions of leadership. They retain as a shadow the vestige of the former self and former Christ light, yet even that shadow of their former days of glory does place them above their peers in many fields.

Thus, it has fallen upon the messengers of this century and now upon the Mother of the Flame, who speaks before you, to continue the work of going after the one million.

Many of these are self-satisfied in their accomplishments, in their attainments, and yet they do not return to their former devotion to the Lord Christ. Others [not of the one million] have come forward to take up the calling to be his disciples and in measures of devotion have outdistanced the original remnant. Yet in ancient times that remnant did have greater attainment than that to which the newer followers of Jesus have attained.

Thus, beloved, the teachings of the ascended masters, given freely, are a specific transfer, a quickening and a knowledge unto those who had them 35,000 years ago in the golden age of Atlantis and in many centuries prior to that; for those souls had been with Jesus long before the fullness of their time came in that golden age.

Therefore understand that the traditions found in the Western Bible contain fragments of this ancient teaching. These fragments have been filled in by the ascended masters today, your beloved Saint Germain, your El Morya and, of course, the Lord Jesus Christ. Many others have joined them until the saints robed in white in numberless numbers[3] have come forward to give this teaching not only to those who had it long ago but also to those who will take it up now as a new study, for they are newer souls and have not had this background that the older souls have had.

The souls who have been on earth for tens of thousands of years and more are familiar with the teaching even if they were not a part of this remnant of the one million. And therefore, when those for whom this teaching is a reading of the Law written in their inward parts[4] come to our meetings and receive the teaching, they instantly confirm it by the ancient record that is written in their own book of life.*

Others who are newer souls, coming more recently to earth, know Jesus only in the more modern sense of the word and they are frightened by the ancient mysteries and the power of the I AM THAT I AM. They know not the intonation of the Word and are not familiar with the sounds that were heard in the temples of Atlantis. Thus, decreeing to them is anathema. They see it as devil worship and they fear even the sight of the Lord Shiva, whom they perceive as some ancient god that rivals "their Jesus."

Jesus does take these souls to temples of light in their finer bodies during sleep to instruct them, but often their fear of the unfamiliar, together with their indoctrination, is too great and when they return to outer consciousness they are not able to adapt to the path that you have been taught.

By the dispensation of Saint Germain and the Goddess of Liberty, freedom of religion has been guaranteed in America even though that guarantee has been violated horrendously by kidnappings, by deprogrammings, reprogrammings and brainwashing, and by all manner of treachery and intrigue.

Thus you see the movements of the Chaldeans and the black priests of Atlantis come again to snuff out the true path of Saint Germain and Jesus Christ. They come to turn the people against that path, and the people unwittingly follow them and know not that in following them they are again rejecting the mighty one of old, the living Jesus Christ, the great emperor of the golden age of Atlantis.

Those black priests who have come again to tear the children from the breast of Jesus are the very same ones who turned the Atlanteans against Jesus and caused them to demand his resignation and withdrawal from the continent. Such a rejection of the Son of God is surely an infamy. And today these ones, who try again to turn the little ones

*the book of the records of their comings and goings and their karma

and more advanced souls against him, shall know that the hour of their judgment is come.

May you be as wise as these serpents and not be overtaken by them, for they attempt to take from you your lawful path of personal Christhood. May you also understand, beloved, that the poison that goes forth from the lips of these who would destroy the path of the ascension for the many is a poison that colors the mind for many for years to come.

May you pray and decree, as you have been taught, that this interference from the voices of the night, which is once again severely compromising the rising of the Mother flame and the coming again of a golden age of Aquarius under the leadership of Saint Germain and Jesus Christ, be stopped.

Now understand, beloved, that I sought with all of my heart to bring the ancient Suernis into a love and a devotion of the Divine Mother. For it is the Divine Mother who gives the attainment and the mastery and the raising up of her light whereby the individual may have mastery over himself, his circumstances and the elements, and may command the forces and the elementals. Beloved ones, this experiment was such a disaster that not since then has a high adept ever been empowered in a position of rulership to compel adherence to the moral code of the conserving of the sacred fire.

To this day, then, the option for self-mastery is left to the freewill decision of everyone upon earth. The decision of how to spend the light of the crystal cord descending from the I AM Presence and the light of the Divine Mother rising upon the spinal altar remains the province of every individual in the privacy of his personal counsel with God.

That is not to say, however, that the individual who does choose to continue to squander that light in lasciviousness and all manner of lust is free of the karma of so doing, for the light belongs to God: it is the descending light of Alpha and the rising light of Omega.

Thus, the path of adeptship is open to all. As you have been counseled to seek power and empowerment for the healing of the nations and for the saving of these cycles of opportunity in the last days of the age of Pisces, so I counsel you that the raising up of this light by pure love and devotion to the Trinity and the Divine Mother will give you that power which you so desire.

The question is: Will you desire that power enough to allow yourself to be weaned from its misuses and the scattering and the diminishment of your forces?

So, beloved, this is the question that is upon you. Those who love much and are much loved, of them much is expected and they expect much of themselves. And because their love of Jesus is so great, they are able to wield the power of the sacred fire and through mantra and meditation to arrive at the place where their chakras are always filled, their lamps are trimmed, and they have the wherewithal to transfer a light to those in whom the fire has gone out.

With what light, then, shall the fire be rekindled in those who have let it go out?

May it be with your light but may its transfer be always by the permission and under the jurisdiction of Jesus Christ. The oil of your lamps is a sacred gift and it must be given only to those who are worthy and committed in its use, else you will find yourself running out of your own light by distributing it without discrimination.

My desire, then, was so very great, and I did learn the lessons of too much love and how too much love for the child, in giving so much, does spoil the child. And therefore this evolution of Suernis who were under me have remained in that state of being spoiled and self-indulgent and have, many of them, remained stubborn and stiff-necked children to the present.

Though they were under the guru Moses, though they were under Abraham and the patriarchs, though they have had many opportunities —visited by the archangels and by servants of God who have dotted the centuries as the Sons of the Solitude come again and again—yet in this day, still in rebellion against those ancient days of my love, they insist upon the misuse of the sacred fire as a continued defiance *of me personally!*

They have never forgotten or forgiven me in my attempt to convince them to restrain their uses of the sacred fire, whereby they might be empowered not only to command the energies for the conveniences of life but, of course, to enter into a path that would bring them ultimate reunion with God.

Thus, they have denied that reunion and used what powers remain with them of that ancient time as a shadow of a former self to sustain a civilization of materialism and to ensconce themselves in positions of power, protected now not by the sacred fire or their adeptship but by money itself. Thus, money has become their god and they have used that money as power to control peoples and nations and economies and banking houses. Understand, beloved, just how great can be the resentment of a people toward their God.

Now, therefore, I come to you to ask your assistance. For I desire, of course, once again to woo the reincarnated Suernis to a path of love, to an inner awakening; for many of them, though they yet carry their anger, suffer from depression.

It is a deep depression, for they know at unconscious levels of being that in my person and in the persons of other Sons of the Solitude they have lost the truest friend they ever had. They know that they do not have that tie to the living Christ and yet they do not desire to surrender their substance,* to bend the knee, to confess that they have espoused the golden-calf consciousness and civilization, and to leave all this behind them for the love of the mighty one of God, the Lord Christ.

Thus, it is an hour when you see a karma repeated again and again. The cycles of opportunity to overcome the repetition of this karma are coming to a close for the Suernis. When I speak of the Suernis, I am not speaking of the one million souls who yet have the option to take that ascension but of the rebellious ones who embodied through them as the Suernis who rebelled against me.

Thus, understand that that rebellious generation must know that their time is short, ultimately, to receive their God. They shall not have to deal with me, for God has withdrawn me from their scene. I, having done all I could do, see that I am but a stone of stumbling in their path.

Thus, it has been given to them to know other Sons of the Solitude even today. May you pray for the reincarnated Suernis as you have been taught, for the powerful calls you give[6] are the only means whereby they may be set free from a dweller-on-the-threshold that, person by person to the last man and woman, is a giant of gargantuan

*their misqualified energy and their misuses of the sacred fire[5]

stature that they are ill-equipped to deal with. In fact, most have embodied that not-self as their personhood instead of embodying the Holy Christ Self.

Adeptship today, then, is by free will. Alas, the Path is not prominent in the West. Many have never heard of such a path or, if they have, fear it as something that they would call occult. As you know, *occult* simply means "hidden," that which is the hidden wisdom that is unveiled to the initiate.

But there is a path, beloved, and it is under the ascended masters. And since my ascension I have been able to work with many who have lovingly received my ministration and who have desired the techniques of full God-mastery for one reason and one alone: the purest love of God and the desire to help his own. Thus, I have graduated to the place of being able to work with those who are certainly suffused with the love of Christ and therefore can make rapid and light strides on this path of progress.

May you know, then, that individual by individual, as you have been told, the Path is most personal and many of you are reaching the place where you may have a very personal transfer from us through the messenger. May you understand that it is according as* you fulfill the Law.

No more will be spoken to you of the matter. You will prepare yourself inwardly and make yourself ready, bearing in mind that often karma alone stands between you and a more accelerated path of initiation. Thus, the violet flame must never be set aside for some other occupation. It is your key to the kingdom of God.

I, too, am grateful that the story of my involvement in the land of Suern has been recorded in the book by Phylos the Tibetan, for with the understanding of my experience many will see that to force the issue of the path of spirituality [or celibacy, using the sacred fire only for procreation], is not wise. This includes not forcing the spiritual path upon children but rather acquainting them with their options and allowing them to choose when [or if] they desire to make a more than ordinary commitment to the Path.

**according as* (16th-century usage): in accord with the way in which; depending on how; depending on whether

Thus, beloved, the greatest teacher is the best example. I sought to be that example in that land of Suern and the record shows that I did succeed.

Nevertheless, the example unto those who want none of it is never sufficient; but the record that is left in akasha of your example will always be there. And you will rejoice to see from inner levels and other octaves as you move on in your journey to the Sun how souls will come along and suddenly find themselves locked in the replica of your Electronic Presence that you have left along the byways of life. Locking in to the record of your being, they will suddenly rejoice in gladness and know that the day has come for their intimate and personal association with an unascended or ascended master who will take them all the way to the point of their God-realization.

Thus in this life you have been reconnected to your I AM Presence by the grace of someone. The outer contact is one thing but the dispensation for that contact comes from the ascended realms and the levels of the archangels. Therefore give gratitude where gratitude is due—to God for the dispensation you have been given for the opportunity of receiving this teaching.

Each day many across the world encounter one of the books or *Pearls of Wisdom* or someone who knows the Path, and they feel as though their life has just begun and their search has ended. And thus, they move with a holy zeal to recapture the lost years and to enter in to the closest communion with our bands that they can accomplish in this life.

Knowing, then, how precious is the gift and how much you have valued the teaching, realize that you were given a long time of being apart from that path and teaching so that you could long for it and yearn for it and desire it, so that you could see the futility of all other paths—all of this so that when you came in contact with this path there would be no turning back and no compromise.

Yet still there are those who when they discover the rigors of self-discipline and the sacrifices that are simply part of the Path, and the surrender and the need for service, et cetera, do turn back and say, "It is too hard."

I counsel you that when as parents or teachers you make life too easy for children and their studies too easy and you do not give them hurdles so that they might develop levels of excellence and a sense of accomplishment in the mastery of self, you fail to prepare them for the reality of the rigors of the true path of life.

Children love a good struggle and a hearty accomplishment. Give them the freedom, then, to have this experience and they will easily walk in the footprints of Jesus or a Saint Francis or one of the many saints and they will move on. When they exercise and build their lungs and their bodies and develop strength in sports as well as in hard work, they will not consider the Path arduous but simply the next challenge to be encountered.

So, my beloved, I have come to speak with you this evening that you might know my heart and know the gentleness of my love that forever loves you and only desires, if you will have me, to assist you in your personal adeptship even as I would have assisted the Suernis centuries ago but was refused en masse by the people.

I am certain you understand the sorrow I had then. I wish to make certain that you understand the joy I have today, for there are so many grateful students. I am glad to participate in the doings of the Darjeeling Council and with the Brothers and Sisters of the Golden Robe under Koot Hoomi. I am grateful to be counted among those who may assist the willing.

Praise God that you are the willing hearts! In that willingness, I bid you to your full God-mastery in this life. May you enjoy a period of adeptship and may you see how much you can give to people once you have been willing to discipline your soul and your energies to that end.

Therefore I bow to the light of God shining upon the altar of your being. May it increase! May it increase. And may your love of the Divine Mother be the key to the mastery of the four quadrants of her Matter universe.

In the bliss of the Spirit cosmos, I take my leave of you. But I am on call as is every ascended master; and by law, the law of love, your love and my love, I must respond. I can do naught else.

October 13, 1991
New Orleans, Louisiana

CHAPTER 8

Lord Shiva

THE POWER OF CHANGE

The Action of the Holy Spirit in Your Life

Lo, *Shiva!* is come to you! Now come to my heart and know the fire of the Holy Spirit, the fire of the ruby ray.

I AM the power of change. Depending on whether or not you desire change, you can surely have it—change from the mortal to the immortal, the corruptible to the incorruptible.

It is only a question of your desire, for desire is *Shiva!* in action in your life. Desire is the telling of that which you shall draw unto yourself. By your desiring, the Law must fulfill that which you desire. Thus, see what you have drawn to yourself, what you have repelled, what you can be and what you are not, and determine if you desire to have *Shiva!* in action in your life.

Know me and know my Shakti, for by the power of the feminine force is light gone forth. Light shall redeem. Light shall always extinguish itself in those who misuse it, for light is God and not mere energy. *Light, Light, Light* is the activating force of our twin flames of the Holy Spirit in action in you!

Let me make it plain and simple. What you are and have today of God and light is by your desiring and your choosing. God will not withhold anything from thee, my beloved, if you are willing to pay the price for the gift for which you ask. It is as simple as that.

Desire the scepter of power to heal a world and be willing to give ten times more of the misuse of power that you have recorded in your lifestream in order to get that scepter.[1] To give up something is the need of the hour. When you go to the altar, tell God what you will give of your misqualified energy as well as your propensity to misqualify it in order to get what you would get. Let the divine interchange take place, rags for riches. God is on the short end of the bargain, but in the end he will have you and himself in you, all of you.

So, beloved, write your list. It is more than a Santa Claus list. It is the determination of your life from this moment to the hour of the last breath. Ponder the breath. In and out perpetually, by the heartbeat the breathing does continue. But one day the last breath is drawn and then expelled.

Know this, then, that as the hairs of thy head are numbered, so thy breaths are numbered. The breathing in and the breathing out is the rhythm of Alpha and Omega and the coming and the going of the Son of God, who is the beginning and the ending of your life.

Choose this day whom you will serve[2] and see how your master becomes your servant. Serve the light and the light will turn and serve you. Serve the darkness and the darkness will turn and control you until you are in its grips and cannot extricate yourself. And depending on whether you have a prior karma of good momentum, you may or may not receive assistance.

No one does knowingly allow himself to be put in the jaws, the yawning jaws, of darkness. Yet each day people make choices to bind themselves to descending spirals, thinking "a little bit—a little bit will not hurt."

I tell you, many drops make up the power of the Ganges, many drops, beloved. Thus drops of darkness create the river in hell. Thus you know Styx. Thus you know the fallen ones. They themselves are prisoners of the darkness they have espoused and put upon the youth of the world.

Choose, then, a straight and narrow path. Come to Mount Kailasa![3]

Come to the heights of the Himalayas! Know my consort and know me, for we are indeed archetypes of your twin flames.

The path to God is easy. I say it. It is true.

Set the eye and the heart. Set the jaw and the gait. Lock yourself in to that path. Determine not to stray from it and you will find that by remaining constant to your vow it is not difficult. For in the constancy of the vow, beloved, all other momentums are starved. You no longer feed them your life force. They begin to dry up as an old snakeskin and wither away in the wind.

I AM Shiva! I am always nigh at hand. I pursue, as the hound of heaven, the students on the path of the initiates of the East and of the ascended adepts. You do not need to call me with a long and loud call as if I were far away! A simple signal will suffice, for I am the genie of the ruby ray. I am always ready, beloved.

Turn your life around with me and I will show you my cosmic dance, and I will dance with you and whirl in the sphere of fire. Yes, I shall show you how imminent is your victory.

Set forth your desirings. Then make your life a one-pointed goal to achieve them. Nothing shall be impossible to you with God as Brahma, Vishnu, and *Shiva!*

Notice how in my aura you can fully believe what I am saying, for I hold a geometric matrix that does strengthen your mind and will and heart and body.

In this moment you know that you *can.* You know that you will walk and dance and sing with me and Shakti all the days of your life! And you will have such a victory that on the way you shall also bind the Chaldean armies. You shall also know the company of saints and angels. All this is possible to you in God and you know it in this moment. Therefore I inscribe it upon your soul.

I strengthen you, beloved, now by the ruby fire. May you desire to retain it, for the Law allows me to sustain this presence about you only for a certain length of time and breadth of space.

Thus, beloved, my message is clear. It is a powerful and loving and wise one. It is the message of one who has followed and led your course for centuries and millennia.

I AM the eternal manifestation of the Holy Spirit. I AM one with the Maha Chohan. If you prefer to call to him, by all means do so, for I shall still be answering the call.

The threefold flame in your heart is the personification of Brahma, Vishnu, and Shiva. You can see those three plumes as ourselves personified. Then you may talk to us. We are not a three-headed god, beloved, but Three-in-One, for we also have a threefold flame. Thus, threefold flame again and again repeated throughout eternity does find us in the heart of every son and daughter of God.

It is well for a time to visualize us personally rather than simply as an impersonal flame that is burning. Meditate upon us not as statues or pagan gods but as the very fire and the replica of the Godhead that has been placed in your heart.

Feel the presence of that light now, for it does become a weight and the preponderance of the weight of God himself. Know this weight for a moment in your chest cavity, as that weight is heavy as the world itself in the heart of the messenger.

Know that God has presence and power and such a weight of dominion that you can feel it even as a weight in the body. But this is but for a moment so that you can establish some sense of co-measurement as to how you will remember us, how you will see us and how you will know that we also merge as one in the single unfed flame of sacred fire, even the Maxin Light[4] that burned on the altar of Atlantis.

Yes, beloved, all returns to the One and the fire infolding itself. All is available to you.

Now, will you call for the Holy Spirit's action in your life? [Audience replies, "Yes!"] Now will you remember that the response is instantaneous and that I am there?

I come also, beloved, with a new dispensation of momentum. By that which is achieved, I do personally sponsor this movement and organization at the culmination of its thirty-three years. Yes, I, Lord Shiva, shall multiply the gifts and graces of the sponsoring masters and the chelas in embodiment by my presence, by my flame.

O ribbons of ruby fire, reach now to the farthest reaches of the earth and beyond! Let ruby ribbons be tied to the hearts of those who yearn for the ruby ray and for love and for this path and for the return and to be done with all of the momentum of rebellion and resentment of the Suernis.

Oh yes, beloved, I am a dissolving fire. And those who are not ready for the fire of the Holy Spirit ought best prepare for it, for the Maha Chohan has already announced in California the descent of the Holy Spirit's judgment.[5] No one can stand the fire of the Holy Spirit in that judgment who has not filled himself with that fire and who does not meet it fire for fire!

Yes, beloved, I counsel you, shirk not the responsibility, avoid not the opportunity to invoke the ruby ray. For it shall stand and still stand, and you shall stand with it and in it in the day when others cannot survive their karma, for they have not prepared to meet their God in the Lord *Shiva* that I AM, *Shiva* that I AM.

I am preparing you for all things. And it is my presence that shall enable you to make a decision, even this night, to go for the power of God and the transmutation of all of its abuses, to gain that empowerment and stand and still stand before all of the challengers of that power who come to you.

You might as well, beloved, for sooner or later you must deal with the eventuality that you will need to seek power, because power is a necessity in order for you to move on in the spirals of the ascension. But when you receive power, you will be assailed by the fallen ones who have stolen the power of God.

You will meet them sometime, somewhere. Why not do it in the eternal Now, have done with it and confirm before all of them that you stand one with God and therefore you fear not their dire threatenings?

Yes, my beloved, this is a day at hand when many can support you. Take it! For I see the days ahead when this initiation shall come to you not by choice but by the cycles having turned whereby you no longer have a choice. And in that day, beloved, you shall not know such a support team as you find today in the ascended hosts, the unascended brethren, the community, the messenger and the group dynamics of your decrees.

Take it, I say! Take it! For I AM Shiva! I am not a beggar, yet I have come almost begging tonight.

Rather, then, in the power of the ruby star I speak, I seal, I love, I reach out, I hold, I bear, I AM the magnet of the ruby ray of the Central Sun!

I AM Shiva!

In the name of the living Christ, so command and I comply.

Thou art sealed now. This sealing will last a certain time, giving you the option to seal your vow. Make your pact with me, beloved, for we have many worlds to conquer and devils to dismiss permanently.

C'est tout! Voilà. C'est fini. [73-second standing ovation]

October 13, 1991
New Orleans, Louisiana

Lord Shiva is the incarnation of the Holy Spirit, the Lord of Love whose whirling cosmic dance dispels ignorance and the forces of anti-love. He is the Third Person of the Hindu Trinity—Brahma (the Creator), Vishnu (the Preserver), and Shiva (the Destroyer/Deliverer)—which parallels the Western Trinity of Father, Son, and Holy Spirit. Shiva is known as the Destroyer/Deliverer because his all-consuming love, when invoked in the planes of Matter, binds the forces of evil and transmutes the cause and effect of man's miscreations, thus delivering him from the prison house of karma. He is the "fearsome one" who drives away sin, disease, death, and demons of delusion. Shiva's action is crystallized in the world of form through his Shakti, or feminine counterpart, who appears in various forms. As Parvati ("Daughter of the Mountain") she is the beneficent, gentle mother and wife. As Durga ("Goddess Beyond Reach") she is the fierce defender of her children, terrible and menacing to her enemies. As Kali ("Power of Time") she appears with a terrifying countenance, shattering delusions of the ego and destroying ignorance.

Shiva is the cherished friend of the chela in distress. On April 24, 1978, he asked us to use his name as a fiat of light:

> There is no need to go around being burdened by the consciousness of the fallen ones. I say, invoke *Shiva!*... You have but to call, to speak my name, to exercise that name.... Repeat it often. Speak it to the wind and to the sky, speak it into the subway and to the trains that pass you by. Shout it into the waves of the sea. Speak it in the night and in the day. It is a fiat of light. I give it to you as a dynamic decree. Let the full momentum of the wind and the breath of the Holy Spirit be that joy within you. And when you say it, *jump* and say, *"Shiva! Shiva! Shiva!"*... See how the fallen ones tremble! See how... the blood will flow and how your heart will expand, and suddenly you will be stumping throughout the land, and you will see that Shiva will have a thousand million faces and be in a thousand million places through you and you. And you will do my cosmic dance, and you will dance upon the demons of your own ignorance and in *joy* you will overcome! So let it ring throughout the earth: *Shiva! Shiva! Shiva! Shiva!*

(See Shiva, 1978 *Pearls of Wisdom,* vol. 21, no. 37. Also *Shiva! Sacred Chants from the Heart of India* and *Sacred Songs from the Heart of India: To Krishna, Ganesha and Surya;* both available on CD from Store.SummitLighthouse.org.)

CHAPTER 9

Saint Germain

The Golden Cycle of the Central Sun 1

LIGHT CYCLES OF THE DECADE

A Scientific Plan for Individual Victory

Hail, Keepers of the Flame and lovers of freedom's light! I, Saint Germain, enter the city and the citadel of your consciousness.

Welcome! [27-second standing ovation. Congregation gives the salutation:] *Hail, Saint Germain! Hail, Saint Germain! Hail, Saint Germain! Hail, Saint Germain! Hail, Saint Germain! Hail, Saint Germain! Hail, Saint Germain! Hail, Saint Germain! Hail, Saint Germain! Hail, Saint Germain! Hail, Saint Germain! Hail, Saint Germain!*

Now out of the Light[1] of the Central Sun I release the golden cycle of the sun, and its release in this hour is timed according to the cycles of the Great Causal Body. Therefore, beloved, prepare to receive that cycle as it descends to earth. Thus, be seated that I may speak to you of its portent.

The golden cycle of the sun is a release of Light out of the very sphere of the golden light of the crown chakra. Thus, it does come for the increase of the power, the wisdom, and the love of the mind. Therefore, let the Holy Trinity be also ensconced in that mind of God in you.

This is a spiral, beloved, that shall affect all evolutions of the Matter cosmos according to the cycle of their individual worlds and planes.

The cycle therefore lends itself to the cycle already commenced by the individual initiate.

Inasmuch as you have heard a great deal about the path of the initiate and the chela, know that it is to the purpose of your fulfillment of this path that certain dispensations are forthcoming in this decade. They are concurrent with the dark cycles of karma but they are the light cycles of the causal bodies of the saints. And these light cycles, like unto the golden cycle of the Great Central Sun, converge; and those who are ready and those who are prepared, even as those who did receive the planting of the seed in the chalice prepared,[2] *they* shall know a great boon of Light.

For as darkness comes forth to be balanced (i.e., transmuted), so light does come forth. As a man soweth, so shall he also reap. Therefore now is the hour, and continuing, to reap the golden cycle of the sun of your causal body that you have sown into the various planes of the universe in all of your sowings since you left the Great Central Sun with your twin flame.

Thus, it is the hour of the reward of the prophets and of the saints[3] and of those who have come as the messengers and the instruments of God, and that release of Light shall be an empowerment that they themselves have generated. Thus you have access, as of this day, to certain cycles, specifically golden cycles of the sun of your own Presence that have returned to you by the good works that you have sent out.

I AM Saint Germain. I, then, come as the facilitator of this process. For I place my violet flame between the soul and causal body of the one who is servant on the seventh ray with Melchizedek, king of Salem and priest of the Most High God, with Zarathustra, with Lord Zadkiel, with the Elohim Arcturus and Victoria, with my own mentor, the Great Divine Director.

You who have served the seventh ray in the temples of Lemuria and Atlantis and other planetary homes even as far away as the Violet Planet, you now have that boon of the violet flame that I may multiply. I multiply your portion and increase it. And therefore between your soul and your causal body is violet flame; and by and through that violet flame, the golden cycle of the Great Central Sun and of your causal body can quicken the crown chakra, can quicken your soul and quicken your entire manifestation.

It is up to you, beloved. Because it is you, the individual, who determines what you can receive. It is the individual lodestone. It is the individual momentum. By your momentum, by your fruits, by all that you bring to this table prepared in the wilderness, so shall you receive.

As though it were awards night, beloved, so there does come to you opportunity—opportunity according to cycles. These cycles are foreordained in the beginning of the *manvantara,*[4] in the beginning of the outbreath of God. Thus, in the inbreath all cycles return to the point of beginning, which is also the point of ending.

Now I say, beloved, there are portents, some that are positive, such as the handwriting in the skies portending the coming of avatars and Christed ones to be born under the auspicious astrology of Pluto exceeding its outer ring and moving toward the center of the solar system within the orbit of Neptune. So you see, beloved, there is that Light. And as there is that crossing, so there can be the crossing over of lightbearers of tremendous dimension whose causal bodies coincide with the golden cycle of the sun.

Therefore look to the hour of the Divine Manchild appearing in many a babe and in the Christ Self of you. Look to the Divine Mother within you, each one, to give birth to that Christ consciousness. Look to yourself to increase in devotions to the Divine Mother that you might ever be her presence within the earth.

Yes, beloved, unto the beginning and the ending of ages there is the coming of great avatars. Whether they shall succeed in this era depends upon the vigilance of all lightbearers, in the first instance, as they call for the binding of Antichrist that does oppress and oppose these children and, secondly, in the very protection of the children themselves.

It was a period of great darkness when the word did go forth from the mouth of Isaiah concerning the prophecy of the coming of the child. The child that was to come was a child in that era and in succeeding centuries leading unto the culmination of the birth of the avatar Jesus Christ.[5]

I, therefore, make known to you this unleashing of the golden cycle of the sun as opportunity for you individually to bring forth fruits from your causal body that have not been accessible to you in this life nor in previous lifetimes lest you should misuse them or squander that treasure.

Now the hour is come to those who have some degree of self-discipline, who have grown wiser by many mistakes and many right decisions. In that point of wisdom may you cherish, then, that treasure from your own causal body and cherish even more the fact that from the Great Central Sun there can be released to you these positive momentums of a cosmos.

I, Saint Germain, come to you, then, not alone for the inauguration of this spiral, as it has been appointed to me by God to so inaugurate it, but I come also as the figure of the prophet in the land.

I also come grateful for the readings given by the messenger, for the facts presented, grateful that these may reach some numbers through avenues open to you. For, beloved, in order for me to quicken minds and hearts with the truth, there must be some trickling of the facts into those minds and hearts—facts that provide knowledge as coordinates already present in their minds so that they might understand the truth when they hear it.

It is a time to multiply the power of the violet flame by returning to the vigil of the All-Seeing Eye of God and Cyclopea's decree.[6] It is a time to invoke the All-Seeing Eye and to concentrate your forces at the point of the brow. Without vision, surely the people of this nation shall perish! And there is not vision among the leadership. And if there is vision in some places, it is denied in preference to the wishful thinking, the illusory thinking, that has pervaded the land.

There are layers and layers of consciousness in the leadership as well as in the people—levels of fear of death and hell, fear of the consequences of facing reality. This fear has become of such great proportion that it is paralyzing the minds even of those who do know better.

A great gamble is being taken by the leadership of this nation and of the Soviet Union. And those who stand to lose most are those who have most, both of freedom and of the technology of this world and of a civilization unparalleled since certain times on Atlantis.

Yes, America stands to lose, beloved, and she shall lose mightily unless there be a clearing of the fog, a parting of the veil and the recognition that America remains vulnerable and more vulnerable with each passing day; for that vulnerability has to do with the passing of cycles of time and of opportunity to take action.

Soon that time will run out if it has not already. For the mobilization of forces in the spiritual defense, the psychological defense, the military defense of a nation and a people and of an entire free world does require cycles of time.

I speak to you, then, of the dispensations of the violet flame announced by Omri-Tas and me.[7] These dispensations you have used, though not to the utmost or the ultimate. Therefore you have gained what has been gained, and in a personal sense some have made marked progress. On the other hand, beloved, there is such a layered effect of deceit across the nations of the world that it will take much, much more effort on your parts to transmute that deception as it grinds out from the mills of those who have become the world's masters of deceit.

I will add, then, to the statements of the messenger that there is much, much more that is hidden that must be revealed. Your calls to Cyclopea can bring this information before the public, and the facts we have at hand can be made known.

You must, then, pray diligently for the transmutation of fear and doubt on the part of the people and their leadership that they will have the courage to stand midst the people, regardless of the consequences to their position, their name or their fame, to speak the facts and to speak truly of the grave conditions both in the economy and in the military.

I have been the sponsor of this nation and I have sponsored a way of life, a civilization, a flame of freedom and the initiation of every soul who does come to this land by the power of the Goddess of Liberty. And that initiation has been the key to the reigniting of the threefold flame and the opportunity for every soul who is of the I AM Race to pursue a path of personal Christhood through discipleship under Jesus Christ.

Now, therefore, beloved, America is truly the cradle of a new age, one that ought to become a golden age. I ask you to consider well how you can fulfill your role, as it has been your destiny since you were embodied on Atlantis to come to this nation to give of your heart and causal body and to arrive at a certain spiritual attainment.

If there can be some—the few, the thousands, the ten thousands—who will rise up to take this path and teaching to apply it to themselves and their own self-mastery that they might stand as pillars in the land, having accomplished at least their individual and personal victory, then I will yet have something to say before the Lords of Karma when I go before them for grants of dispensations for the saving of this civilization.

Alas, it is late in the centuries, and some of those who have come to be reborn here to build America in this century and the last have not fulfilled their reason for being. Some have entered into the same old Atlantean spirals of deception, the abuse of power and money, and have therefore turned around what might have been truly by this day a golden age in America. Blessed ones, if we cannot see the thousands rising up in the near future, then let us at least see that some sons and daughters of God come Home having fully accomplished their assignments.

I know that the desire is upon your heart to know and understand what God has appointed you to do in this life and in previous lifetimes. I know that you have a deep desiring to fulfill all things so that you might arrive at the gate of the next world having fully accomplished your mission.

I can assure you that the violet flame will assist you in accelerating both that mission and those spirals of light that are in every atom and cell of your being. I assure you that you can encapsulate time and accelerate time and that you will find yourself accomplishing in ten years what without the violet flame could take you a century.

The violet flame does shorten the distance between you and the bonding of your soul to the Sacred Heart of Jesus. It does increase the capacity of every moment and hour. It accelerates the functioning of the mind and the ability of the body to be rejuvenated.

If you look for the elixir of eternal youth, I tell you it is the violet flame. Drink of it daily! If you look for the regeneration of certain parts of the body, if you look for the revitalizing of the mind and heart and even for the spiral of the resurrection flame to enfold your entire being, invoke the power, wisdom, love of the Trinity and call forth showers upon showers upon showers of living violet flame of the seventh ray.

Know and discover, then, the alchemy of the Spirit. Do not lament lost hours or years or days but know that from this moment of the eternal Now, you can live in eternity while yet walking the earth in these forms you yet wear. You can be renewed each day and you can walk that perfect path because of the violet flame and because of the golden cycle of the sun that is unleashed in this hour.

Yes, beloved, all things are possible to you in God. Therefore "get right with God," as they say. Establish the plumb line of Truth.

Determine that you shall be wed to your Holy Christ Self by a certain day and date and set a reasonable timetable for yourself. Then call for the initiations of Jesus Christ and ask that you might be made his very personal disciple and that he might anoint you this night. Set yourself to the task of rooting out, plucking out, line by line and hair by hair, every point that is out of alignment with that Christ-potential within you.

If you are determined and *absolutely determined* on this path and you will not take a backward step but pass every test, I, Saint Germain, assure you that you can make rapid strides in the internal harmony of being and in the great fount of love that wells up within you, even as a gift of the Sacred Heart of Jesus to you. And I assure you that you are now able to achieve that bonding much more quickly than you have anticipated.

Most individuals do not have more than five seriously bad habits in their worlds. You should isolate what you consider to be five negative practices or habits, character traits or momentums that you notice are repetitive in your life.

Isolate them. Go after them. Call to the Five Dhyani Buddhas to help you! Call to Mighty Cosmos' five secret rays to help you! Go after the eradication of those points, beloved, perhaps points of density or ignorance or slothfulness or untidiness or unkindness, et cetera, et cetera.

When you begin to analyze yourself and set a chart before yourself and write down when you pass or fail your tests, when you will go about this systematically as a grocery packer checks off that which he is packing, as the simplest of workingmen does keep account of what he has accomplished on an assembly line or in any place of work whatsoever—when you look at the spiritual path in these terms, you will find that it is possible to tackle this task with practicality, setting up systems for yourself and reminders so that you can whittle away at the dead and dying momentums of your human consciousness.

This is the way I like to see Keepers of the Flame approach the path of the seventh ray, for it is a path of science and alchemy and the ritual of the cosmos and the ritual of the priesthood of Melchizedek. And divine ritual, beloved, contains within it the formula for its completion from the beginning unto the ending.

I do not like to see you drift idly as the clouds, allowing your consciousness to float hither and yon and not being tethered to the words that we speak to you and not being tethered to the action that must follow in order for us to speak again.

We are precise. We use an economy of words and an economy of energy though we have the entire cosmos at our disposal. Therefore, practice the economy of life and fit into your day those disciplines whereby you feel your mind becoming like steel, you feel the sharper-than-the-two-edged sword in your midst and the dividing of the way of the Real from the unreal.

Set yourself to the task of self-observation. Close your eyes and meditate and take a moment apart, even apart from your body, to look upon yourself as though you were another person. Observe yourself as others observe you. And if you are not able to do this so well, then ask others how they see you or ask to be taken to the Cave of Symbols or to the Royal Teton Retreat, where you may look upon yourself in the cosmic mirror under the guidance of myself or others of the ascended masters who shall tutor you.

Ask and you shall receive! Ask anything that will enable you to be a better servant of God, indeed a selfless servant.

Blessed ones, we are eager to help, for we have much at stake. In many past ages we have pledged our causal bodies, our momentums of Light and all that we are *to your victory.* The possibility of the loss of that victory, therefore, does translate to us as a certain loss of our own invested capital, so to speak, that we have taken from our causal bodies and invested in the lightbearers of the earth.

When you make good on our investment, beloved, I can assure you that we share with you the cosmic returns, and with those returns you may sponsor others and also increase in your own self-mastery.

It is an age of science and nothing can be said to be more scientific than the plan that must be laid by each individual to secure the victory in his individual life and for his nation and for the planet.

It is not an insurmountable problem, this prognostication of war between the superpowers. It is surmountable, but you have to know that it is surmountable. You have to know that the positive good of all of the causal bodies of the Light Beings of a cosmos may combine together in answer to your call to change the course of what might, as of this date, still appear upon the screen of life.

Do not think that the challenge of this war is beyond the ability of the Great White Brotherhood, for I tell you it is not. But unless you get in the driver's seat and see yourself as able—and God in you as able—and see the power of God as greater than all of that might arrayed against the Light of freedom* upon earth, it will not come to pass that this prophecy shall be turned aside.

You must lock in to the posture that you are in God and God is in you and that you are one (for you are his offspring), that Christ the Mediator is the mediator twixt your soul and God and that the violet flame consumes all that is unlike his presence.

I want you to tackle this problem as though it were a neighborhood squabble, for in the entire cosmos this potential war *is* a neighborhood squabble.

Do not misunderstand me, beloved one. The lethal nature of nuclear weapons and those weapons that continue to be built by the Soviet Union is beyond that which the earth has seen in hundreds of thousands of years. Beloved ones, the war that is contemplated can be a horrendous calamity that changes the face of the entire planet. Or it can be won by careful planning.

The combination of minds that lead this nation includes cowards,

*the God consciousness of freedom

deniers, moles from other systems—we call them "enemy aliens"—who are unknown to themselves as moles, and those who, although they have many layers of awareness, are yet willing to take the ultimate gamble. Yes, beloved, the leadership is not strong, but the people themselves have the karma of this poor leadership. Poor leadership, beloved, is a betrayal in itself, and yet many who serve you have long been the betrayers of my lifestream and my flame of freedom and my path of initiation.

Therefore, beware of wolves in sheep's clothing! Beware of forces of Antichrist that move against the flowering of the Christ consciousness in America! At levels of their being they know, beloved, that the reign of peace under Jesus Christ and the power of a golden age and the perpetuation of this path and teaching can only lead to the eventual liberation of every soul of Light and servant of God upon this planet and to the judgment of those who serve the powers of darkness.

Since they also serve the powers of darkness, it is in their interest to preserve chaos and holocaust and war. For by the perpetuation of war, there is the cutting off of the avenue of communication of the teachings, the lost teachings of Jesus Christ, and what they can mean in the personal life of the individual.

Why, beloved ones, do you know that there are many lifestreams upon earth who could—in another decade and another and another, even in the thirty-three-year spiral that is begun for The Summit Lighthouse—if they had this teaching today, actually enter in to that Christhood and be bonded to their Holy Christ Self?

You are living in a time and in an age when many thousands and even millions of people are on the brink of discovering that personal path of Christhood, both within at inner levels and by the contact of this messenger and teaching. Thus you see, beloved, for that reason alone it is in the interest of the powers of death and hell, both those on the astral plane and those in physical embodiment, to stop the very course of civilization and its communication of the word of Jesus Christ, to stop it at any and all costs.

For when these mighty Christed ones rise up and rise up en masse and when the children who are being born and can be born in this decade reach the full age of their maturity, they also shall stand. And therefore, suddenly you shall see tens of thousands and more of souls walking the earth as Christed ones, challenging by the power of the Divine Mother the forces of darkness that have held woman in subjection and have led children astray into all paths of unrighteousness.

Therefore see, beloved, that there is more at stake than the conquest of nations or the taking of territory to perpetuate a Communist world totalitarian system. What is at stake is the very survival of the path of initiation with a continuity into the New Age whereby the teachings are preserved and those aforementioned lifestreams remain in embodiment to pass on to others the momentum of their personal adeptship.

Thus, I have come full circle in my statement to you of the need for personal adeptship. Wherever you may be on the face of the entire earth, you may be the single and solitary one who can demonstrate the path that you have been taught and that you have learned under these messengers.

Thus, beloved, I, Saint Germain, have also walked the earth in time of chaos as the Wonderman of Europe.[8] I have demonstrated a path and a mastery, yet none could relate to it. For the books were not written, the violet-flame dispensation had not come nor the opportunity to give to the masses of the people by mass communication the understanding of the science of decrees. There was no means whereby the rank and file or the royalty themselves could follow a path in my footsteps. All they could have was the stamping upon their memory of my demonstration of alchemical feats.

But did they equate that they might also do this?*

Did they desire to do it?

No, they would rather have the base metals turned into gold. They would rather have the healing of their gems and then have these given back to them than submit to the disciplines necessary to accomplish these feats on their own. Nevertheless, beloved, it was useful to leave the record and many have never forgot the name *Saint Germain.*

Yes, I was the count and I attempted to avert war in that time.

---

*But did they find a point of co-measurement with me whereby they might also do this?

It was not possible, for the heads of state did not lend me their ears nor did they accept my advice when I gave it.

I am in the same position this day, beloved, for I have transmitted to the leadership of the free world and to all those who are servants of Jesus Christ what is the true action that is necessary. They have received this at inner levels in the retreats of the Brotherhood and on certain occasions I have actually manifested to speak to your leaders.

Blessed hearts, they have not received the message. Some have turned a deaf ear. Some have refused to recognize that I am Saint Germain. For one or more reasons of human compromise, I have faced the same response that I faced in the hours preceding the French Revolution. So you understand, beloved, that God abides free will in all octaves and the ascended masters may not force themselves upon embodied individuals, who must play their role on the stage of life as they will.

In addition to myself, many wonderful hearts in many sectors of society, in this activity and outside it, have known what is the true course and recourse in this hour. They have written papers. They have submitted documents. They have introduced bills in Congress. They have spoken on talk shows. Blessed ones, you have gone forth yourselves, and the messenger has delivered the message again and again.

Thus, what does it take for people to accept the truth and see reality?

It takes something more than delivering the message. It takes the decrees to the violet flame to dissolve their doubt and fear, their recalcitrance, their willful nonseeing and the clogging of their minds to the point where they are stupefied and unable to act or move or comprehend something that has become quite complex—and that is the military equation of our time, the equation of the superpowers.

This problem is magnified by the fact that the intelligence services of the West are not revealing to the people what is the truth about what is going on. They have satellites. They have communications networks. They have all manner and means of being able to know what is happening everywhere on the planet.

And yet they have not used this technology that I have released for the purposes to which I have released it: to win the fight for freedom in every nation, to rescue every heart and soul and mind and person who is oppressed, beginning with those who are oppressed in these United States and moving on to those who do not have equal rights and equal opportunity throughout the world.

Blessed ones, there are those who are denied their God-given freedom to be who they are, to worship as they please, to speak and assemble as they please and to publish in the press as they please. Yes, beloved, there are many who are denied freedom of conscience. Truly, many are enslaved by their own momentums and they are enslaved by their karma.

Beloved, I have released a technology that has been used to subvert and pervert the consciousness and the sacred fire of the youth, whether in the amplification of the rhythms of hell in rock music, whether in drugs, whether in purveying across the television all manner of maudlin sentimentality in soap operas and in episodes dealing perpetually with the misuse of the sacred fire and the pastimes of those individuals who are not in any way a part of our bands in that they are not raising the Kundalini. All of this does tear down the moral integrity and the sense of self-worth of the youth, who have high ideals that are at times quickly shattered by these scenarios.

Blessed ones, it is a shame that technology should be used to perpetuate and proliferate a civilization that is decadent and self-indulgent and closing in upon itself. Yes, beloved, it is an hour of narcissism. It is an hour when individuals are in love with themselves. Instead of practicing devotions to God, they preen themselves and their bodies.

And the entire Spirit of the Great White Brotherhood is awaiting those freedom fighters who will indeed champion the cause of freedom in every area of life, beginning with education and the education of the heart, beginning with those fundamentals of life whereby students and children may excel in certain levels and areas of attainment that have to do with the type of native intelligence that they have, God-given.

Search and know the genius of every child, for there is genius in each one. But you must have ingenuity to assist that child to unlock that particular seed of light.

O beloved, what an age, what a *golden* age of Aquarius this golden age can be! How it can be that golden cycle of the sun! And how few it will take to steer the course aright.

I would to God I could empower those of you who know what to do and how to do it! But I may not do so. I may not disrupt the cycles of individual and planetary karma.

You have seen the great heartache of Ernon, Rai of Suern, as he attempted to enforce upon the people those disciplines that should have given them their self-mastery and their own freedom—yet they would not, they would not.[9] And so, many of us have come upon this same resistance as we have desired to assist individuals in the advancement of their adeptship in a given embodiment.

There is a certain stubbornness engrained in the race of mortals, beloved, and all are heir to it to some degree, in that people want to do *what* they want to do *when* they want to do it and not upon the prodding of anyone, least of all an ascended master.

Therefore, always grateful to have your attention, I take this opportunity to place upon your hearts what is on my heart this night. For I love you, and I have come to this city rejoicing that you have come here to challenge the forces of darkness, to cut free the souls of Light and to set a new dimension of that outreach of the Great White Brotherhood.

May you continue from city to city. And may each and every one of you so cherish even a single morsel of truth that you have gained as though it were a leaven, a leaven planted by the Divine Mother in three measures of meal, till it leavens the whole lump of your consciousness.[10] May you be so grateful for that point of truth that expands the mind and heart that you will not rest until you transfer it to those who also seek that morsel of Light.

How precious is a single truth, a single dispelling of Darkness by Light, a single correcting of an error of consciousness, of thought, of doctrine held for lifetimes. Suddenly it is dispelled, evaporated by the violet flame, by the Holy Spirit, by the presence of the Lord Jesus. For the Lord does speak through the messenger and give those lost teachings to you, who may not necessarily hear them by the Holy Spirit. And therefore you hear them by the Holy Spirit of the Lord Jesus Christ speaking unto and through the messenger.

What a wondrous day it is to rejoice and know that Christ is also in you as he is in Jesus!

Wouldn't it be a wonderful pastime, instead of doing a crossword puzzle, to actually sit down and list all of the truths that you have gained by this path and how these truths have been as a bursting of light, as a changing, an elevating, a resurrecting of your being as you have moved on in the cycles of being? And now you are secure on a path whereon you know that as you sow, you shall reap and as you balance karma, so you shall gain the victory and as you move on to the next cycle of the sun, you can win your ascension.

This is the dispensation of Saint Germain unto the lightbearers of this century!

I ask you, beloved ones, those of you who are here or at inner levels, those of you who are of the I AM movement and of all other movements who have taken my name and sponsorship: Will you not consider so great a dispensation and the price that I have paid for it and the price that I have had to pay again and again for certain individuals' misuse of that violet flame?

And will you not realize that you must take this dispensation and multiply it again and again and again that we all might be redeemed and not wind up with the karma of neglect, so that in the very next opportunity when we all go before the Karmic Board, millions of us together, and ask for more violet flame and dispensations for the planet, the Karmic Board shall receive us with open arms and shall say to one and all:

"Well done, thou good and faithful servants of the Most High God and of the seventh ray and of Saint Germain! Thou hast been faithful over the little things, the few things of decreeing daily for the seventh ray to banish darkness in the earth. We shall make thee, one and all, rulers over many." [21-second applause]

In the love and the opportunity and the comfort ever extended to me by my beloved twin flame, Portia, I bid you adieu.

[31-second standing ovation]

October 14, 1991
New Orleans, Louisiana

CHAPTER 10

Omri-Tas

The Golden Cycle of the Central Sun 2

O THE VIOLET FLAME! "I HAVE COME TO GIVE YOU A BOOST!"

Omri-Tas on Planet Earth for 33 Days with 144,000 Priests of the Sacred Fire from the Violet Planet

Out of the Light of the Great Central Sun, I AM Omri-Tas!

And *I AM here!* [32-second standing ovation]

And I have come to give you a boost.

Yes, beloved, I plant myself firmly in the earth, containing the earth in my aura for thirty-three days clocking from this hour. And in this cycle, which is of a purple fire, a purple-golden cycle of the sun, I multiply your decrees to the violet flame specifically for the change in physical conditions on planet Earth—physical conditions in your life, physical conditions pertaining to economic matters, to matters of education and service and life plan and relationships.

It is a cycle, beloved, when you can so liberate your souls by the multiplication of my presence and my further multiplying of the violet flame that I daresay you should not miss a moment to recite a mantra even if it is between thoughts or steps or devotional songs you sing. "I AM a being of violet fire! I AM the purity God desires!" This mantra alone invokes the violet flame and all of my causal body.

You have accomplished what you have accomplished. I desire to see you accomplish more, for you have not yet reached the critical mass where certain elements may melt, where certain world chemicalization may take place that can bring about a greater harmonization of the elements of mind and heart and of peoples. You have not reached that point of the critical mass of the Christ consciousness in the seventh ray.

Would you be as Saint Germain, walking the earth as a Christed One of the seventh ray? [Audience replies, "Yes!"]

It is the calling of the hour and I have come to assist you. Yes, I come to give you a boost. May you please, beloved ones, take advantage of this boost that I might continue to give dispensations, for even I am subject to the cosmic law of karmic, karmic, karmic manifestation.

Yes, beloved, see that you do not make karma with me by failing to take advantage of my proffered gift to you. For I desire to have complete, independent freedom to be able to give to planet Earth in dire moments those dispensations and transfusions of violet flame that are so desperately needed.

Therefore let the violet singing flame sing in your heart! And may you also take up other disciplines in which the violet flame shall assist you, following the instructions that Saint Germain has given you for a scientific path of adeptship.

Therefore, beloved, in gratitude to God apply this opportunity, as you have been grateful for the opportunity of Helios and Vesta[1] and for Helios' dispensations and answers to your calls.

I come as the Ruler of the Violet Planet. And in this thirty-three days, beloved, you may prepare yourselves through saturation of the violet flame so that at the end of that time I may be able to take a company of you to the Violet Planet. It is my desire to take an entire group of souls of planet Earth who are practicing their Ashram rituals and are practicing the Ritual for Transport and Holy Work.[2] We will go on a journey out of the body not to a place on earth for service, which service is of course your vital nightly work, but to the Violet Planet on a journey that I have planned for you who are of this group.

For I desire you to have a firsthand, eyewitness account so that you can bring back from inner levels to those in the etheric octave, as well as to those in physical embodiment, a direct knowledge of events and how they are transpiring and of life on that planet.

Some of you have been there before. Some of you have actually lived there. Some of you have served there with elemental life. Yes, beloved, you shall enjoy seeing what has taken place there since you left.

I desire to show you these things, beloved, so that you can see firsthand and have the record in your being that those things that are projected to manifest on earth need not be and that they are not insurmountable, as Saint Germain has told you. Many conditions that descend as the dire forebodings of plague and the return of the conditions that have happened in earlier centuries[3]—yes, beloved, these things can be transmuted.

I ask you to look for ways and means to accomplish the task, for the violet flame is an ingenious flame and the minds of many ingenious ones have used it for many purposes. I ask you to devise, then, ingenious means whereby you can teach children and people of all ages to sing to the violet flame, to march and clap and dance and even square dance to the violet flame! As long as it is with a mighty rhythm and an action of the correct time, beloved, you can use the violet flame in all sorts of occupations, all sorts of sports and physical exercises.

Cannot the mind act?

Do we not see certain athletes and runners wearing headsets?

Let them hear and know the violet flame. Let them run to the rhythm of it! Let their heartbeats be restored to the action of the threefold time of the waltz in violet flame.

Yes, beloved, there are many physical activities that can be accompanied by joyous shouts of the violet flame and songs not yet written down. There is, therefore, activity in everyone's daily life that can be combined with the violet fire. Let it be a joyous flame, a marching flame, a singing flame, a waltzing flame, a hopping, skipping flame! All the chores that were previously drudgery, let them become spinning wheels of light.

Yes, beloved, you must convert a world to the use of the violet flame if you are to accomplish the hurdle that is before you. Therefore,

I truly say: Seek out the ingenuity of the seventh ray and the violet flame and let it be done quickly.

You are welcome to be seated in the violet flame, which is waiting in your seats. For my angels have placed it there! And it is a cool flame and yet it may seem warm to you, beloved, for it contacts the toxins in your being and the misqualified substance. And until you can feel the coolness, you will feel the warmness and sometimes the hotness! And therefore, do not accuse me of giving you a "hot seat," beloved ones, for it is your own heat of your misqualified substance, and you yourselves have created the hot seat!*

But you have invoked the violet flame and the best is yet to come. For the coolness of that flame is a regulating energy that does keep your four lower bodies in a point of self-regeneration and rejuvenation.

O the violet flame! I shall sing its praises unto the sun!

May you be grateful to work with elementals, for these elementals are whispering to one another and jumping up and down and so happy that you now have the tapes that you can use to bless and heal them. Teach these songs to children and tell them about the elementals. Tell them about the angels. Tell them about their unseen helpers.

The power of the resurrection flame is mighty and therefore on these tapes you weave it with the violet flame. And the weaving of the resurrection flame with the violet flame shall give new impetus to billions upon billions upon billions of elementals of fire, air, water and earth who serve the evolutions of planet Earth. And you shall see *change!* You *shall* see change. *You shall see change.* I say, participate in it and have the prize, the prize of having contributed to that mighty stream.

Visualize the Ganges as a violet-flame river. Visualize the oceans as violet-flame oceans—and all of the waters, even the water that you drink, beloved. Let it become blessed by your hands, left and right, left underneath and right above, as you bless that water and call for it to become your violet-flame elixir.[4]

See the violet flame purging the mind and emptying your cells of those substances that you should never have partaken of in the first place.

*You see, the heat is there because transmutation is taking place, and until you have transmuted an appreciable percentage of the misqualified substance, you will feel heat when you invoke the violet flame or when a great being of light of the violet flame stands in your aura.

Now that you know the correct dietary laws, those promoted by Saint Germain and Morya, may you follow them. For we desire to see eternal youth but you must obey the laws of the physical body to achieve it. And we shall not continue to speak about diet, but we know that you will see that the path of adeptship is, must be, the path of mastery of the four quadrants of being.

Saint Germain has told you that the violet flame is a physical flame[5] and therefore it can and does change physical matter when you cooperate with it. If by free will you violate the laws of physics in your body and the biochemistry, then, beloved, you are working against the violet flame and you will have to live with the consequences of your own free will.

I am gratified that I have been able to place the great reservoir of the violet-flame sea in the center of the earth. Were you to decree twenty-four hours a day, beloved, you would never in a million years exhaust the potential of that sea to multiply your calls. Were every lifestream on planet Earth to give the violet flame twenty-four hours a day, you would still not exhaust the potential of that violet-flame sea to multiply your calls.

Therefore, the greater the number of you who come together in the geometry of God to invoke the violet flame, the greater will be the number of lightbearers you contact through your Ashram Ritual meditations as you visualize the great *antahkarana.** And let that antahkarana be seen as white, as blue, and as violet. Alternate these visualizations. When you desire to see the connection of all lightbearers in the violet ray, then see the antahkarana as a violet filigree. See it strengthened. See it become a mighty net of the Lord our God, even the great dragnet that does bring in all of the "fishes," who are the souls who are ready to return to the mouth of God.

Yes, beloved, there is a wondrous work to do. And there is not a moment in this work that is not a joyous moment when you do it with the violet flame, when you do it with the anticipation of the great return current, when you do it with a confidence that the Law acts.

**antahkarana* [Sanskrit, "internal sense organ"]: the web of life; the net of light spanning Spirit and Matter connecting and sensitizing the whole of creation within itself and to the heart of God

The law of invocation, the science of decrees, is a mathematics all its own. It is a calculus all its own, beloved. And therefore it does not err or fail. And when you put into the computer of the mind of God that exact formula, that exact equation, it shall give back to you that exact formula or that exact equation multiplied by the golden cycle of the sun and by the power of the purple-golden cycle of the sun, which I also bring.

So know, beloved, that this seventh-ray action is a formula that must contain within it not simply a set of numbers or a chemical formula. It is rather a formula of numbers and more—it is a formula of energy vibrations from your chakras, of rays of light, of sacred fire raised up.

You endow your formula with the fire of being. Thus, it is not so simple as writing numbers on a paper. Nevertheless, you have the ability to give this formula, for the key to the formula and to its science is love. And the love of the heart is a twelve-petaled design exact, and these twelve petals are all that is required to construct any formula whatsoever that has to do with the science of the drawing forth of the rays of God from the Central Sun.

Thus, as Jesus taught, when you come to the altar if you have not forgiven brother or sister, if you have not surrendered wrath or anger or hate and hate creation, if you have not sought the purging of your soul and the flame of forgiveness, you must go back and accomplish these things and then come again to the altar.[6] For the altar is the place of change, of alteration, of alchemy, as you have been taught. And to that altar you must come bearing a strong flame of divine love. And as you hold this votive light cupped in your hands, beloved, that flame of love becomes the fire infolding itself that shall manifest the divine formula, and in that formula of love every human need can be met.

Therefore, when you decree, decree in the heart of love. And if you need to decree to get to the heart of love, of course do so. If you need to wield the sword of blue flame and give calls to Astrea, if you need to bathe and change your clothes and feel that you are coming as a supplicant before the altar of God, having performed outer and inner ablutions, then of course do so.

There are many techniques whereby you can bring yourself to that physical and mental strength that will enable you to tarry at the altar and hold a strong flame of divine love. And as your mind's eye is able to see 360 degrees out through the circumference of your aura, wherever you look, no matter what the face, it is divine love manifest as the violet flame that you will send forth through your heart to all—to the just and the unjust, the Real and the unreal, the servant of Light or Darkness.

Let violet flame go forth from your aura! Call to beloved Kuan Yin to place her Electronic Presence over you that by the power of the merciful heart, you may qualify an entire planet with the momentum of mercy as the violet, living flame!

In another vein, I desire you to visualize yourself, picture yourself, constructing with violet flame your own craft—a craft that is able to journey through the sea, through the atoms of the earth, beyond the atmosphere, in interplanetary space and beyond. This craft is an extension of your being, even as your automobile or airplane might be the extension of your being.

You have journeys to take, beloved, that require more than a robe of light. These journeys can be taken by you in crafts that have been constructed by those of our bands. It is time, then, that you understood the laws of creating such vehicles.

By the invocation of the violet flame and the visualization of a spherical or oblong craft, you shall fill in the design and therefore be able to occupy a forcefield of protection that will appear and precipitate as "solid,"* that will contain all the things you need in the unascended state to be away from home for lengths of inner soul travel outside the physical body.

Once you have a conceptualization of this craft, beloved, you simply fill it in each time you give the violet flame. You do not place too much attention upon it, for you know your primary purpose is to dissolve the causes and core of war, to utterly consume and deactivate all harmful weapons, and to foil the plans of the enemy on the astral and physical planes.

You have priorities in the balancing of karma, the purification of

*This vehicle may not be solid in the physical sense.

the planet and, of course, of utmost importance, urgent in this hour, is your service with the elementals. So, beloved, I give you this thought, and thoughtform, that you might tend to it as you are able but not let it become a preoccupying situation in your minds.

Listen in this moment of silence with the inner ear. [5-second pause] I am extending your hearing beyond earth. Listen with your inner ear.

[21-second pause]

As you send forth the extension of the inner ear to contact the sounds of a universe and beyond, notice how you define the known area of the occupation of your mind by the hearing of the inner ear. Where your hearing stops, your sense of space and time also stops. [5-second pause] Thus, visualize the stars and the galaxies and your hearing expanding to the extent of the Milky Way. [5-second pause]

Notice how you transcend the lesser mind and you begin to occupy time and space through the universal mind of God that is in your Holy Christ Self. In reaching for extended hearing, you have also reached for the extended mind of God. When you reach the outer limits of the mental body and yet continue to occupy the mind and extend its occupation, you find yourself making the transition to the mind of God. You do not accomplish this through the brain or through the lower mental body but through the sheer desire and the meditation upon the Christ mind and the intense listening with the inner ear.

If you will enter into this meditation before you retire, you will find that you can strengthen it and extend the hearing power of the inner ear. You can listen to light rays. They have a sound. You can listen to the turning of worlds and stars and suns and planets. They have more than a sound—they have a symphony of sound. You may hear the roaring of the sea, the sea of light, the roaring of the waterfall of light.

And this process will come to you with greater facility as you give the bija mantras to the feminine deities and tune the chakras with the Sanskrit sounds and intonations.[7] The science of mantra will bring you to the heart of mantra in the nucleus of every atom or heavenly body or the point of the seed of light within you.

Yes, beloved, ponder the mystery of life in the moments of quietude and meditation. This is a needed soul nourishment and balance to the daily battle of challenging the forces of Antichrist in the earth. These do assail your messenger, your families, yourselves, your path and your attainment.

Be on guard, beloved, for we have entrusted you with as great a light as you can bear and yet remain protected. Do not fail to invoke the protection of Archangel Michael. Be liberal in your calls to him, erring on the side of more rather than less.

One hundred and forty-four thousand priests of the sacred fire from the Violet Planet have accompanied me for this thirty-three-day sojourn. May you know that we intend to make our mark and to make a difference in the quality of life on earth.

We anticipate and look forward to your fullest cooperation. We desire to see you and the lightbearers and Keepers of the Flame of the earth be able to retain the presence of one such priest or priestess of the violet flame of the seventh ray, to be able to retain it after the thirty-three days of our presence here.

This is an experiment. If you cooperate and take full advantage of it, we shall be able to immediately build upon it and increase and multiply again in the next thirty-three-day cycle.

It might be well for you to put on paper what is your daily pledge to the violet flame and then signify at the end of thirty-three days how you have accomplished it. Write, then, what is your commitment and send it to the messenger. Then send again a letter in thirty-three days informing her as to how you have kept your commitment. By so setting your commitment in writing, written with your own life energy, you shall know the support of violet-flame angels in your fulfillment of that commitment.

Rejoice in the gifts of God, for I do, beloved. And I rejoice most of all in this hour in the gift of you.

I AM and I remain with you, Omri-Tas, saviour of the Violet Planet, saviour of all who would be saved through the path of the seventh ray.

October 14, 1991
New Orleans, Louisiana

Omri-Tas is the Ruler of the Violet Planet. As Saint Germain has told us, Omri-Tas carries such an intensity of violet flame and of the seventh ray in his aura that it extends far beyond the actual size of planet Earth. The evolutions of the Violet Planet have served the violet flame for aeons and use the violet flame to tend to all the needs of daily life—to clean their homes, to care for and purify the planet, and even to wash and bathe in. Menial chores are performed by violet-flame angels and elementals, which allows the people time to pursue the path of adeptship and to serve other planetary homes. Across the Violet Planet, 144,000 priests of the sacred fire tend the violet flame day and night and perform ceremonies and rituals of the violet flame at thousands of altars. Omri-Tas recently told us in his May 1, 1991 dictation that the evolutions of the Violet Planet had once approached a similar crisis as that faced today by the people of Earth. In response to the rallying call of the representative of the Divine Mother, the servants of God were galvanized and turned the tide by the violet flame. As Omri-Tas said: "They heard the call to give their invocations at altars around that planet. There was a saturation of the planetary body with the violet flame. That saturation therefore did flush out the fallen angels, who then could be bound by the legions of light and removed. . . . We went on into a golden age because of the few who responded, and today that planet is sustained in that golden age because the people have not lost the memory of that which was almost a planetary holocaust." (1991 *Pearls of Wisdom,* vol. 34, no. 26, pp. 353–55)

Over the years, Omri-Tas has released specific violet-flame dispensations to assist the chelas of Saint Germain and to uplift the earth. It is important to call to Omri-Tas to reactivate and multiply these dispensations:

Violet-flame spheres. On July 6, 1963, in Washington, D.C., Omri-Tas announced: "Magnificent violet-fire angels from Saint Germain's own band have volunteered to blaze a path through cosmic highways toward the Earth planet and to focus it, beloved ones, upon your nation's capital. . . . The charge of violet fire shall utilize the Capitol dome as an electrode and it shall radiate out as from a great hub throughout the entire planet known as Earth. Every chela of Saint Germain upon this planet shall be blessed with the radiation which we shall pour forth. . . . To complete our great experiment of light we shall now form beautiful, magnificent spheres of violet flame, and we are going to roll them down this cosmic highway in much the manner of a bowler attempting to knock down bowling pins. But we shall hit our mark. There are 144,000 of these spheres. Each one of the priests of the sacred fire here has one in command. . . . For the next twelve hours there shall be a continual release, spaced by cosmic law, of violet flame from this planet." These spheres, visible to the physical sight, were seen by the messengers and students in the sky over Washington following the dictation. (2016 *Pearls of Wisdom,* vol. 59, no. 18)

At Mount Shasta, on July 4, 1975, Saint Germain also spoke of a dispensation of violet-flame spheres from the heart of Omri-Tas: "This night as you watch the release of fireworks, the 144,000 priests of the sacred fire, in their annual release, will send forth the violet-flame balls—those spheres of violet fire—and they will roll those spheres into the earth! And they will also burst! And the fire inside, a sacred fire, will be the anointing of the Holy Spirit to draw a planet unto the victory of light."

Cathedral of Violet Flame. On October 11, 1975, in San Francisco, Archangel Zadkiel announced "the transfer from the priests and priestesses of the Violet Planet of the Cathedral of the Violet Flame." He said: "In this moment it is being transported by angelic hosts as they carry this giant cathedral to be placed in the etheric plane of earth's atmosphere for the consecration of the violet flame and as another focal point for souls desiring to be free to frequent while their bodies sleep at night. And therefore, the Cathedral of the Violet Flame is placed in the heart of the Rocky Mountains in commemoration of the light of freedom of the Ruler of the Violet Planet, Omri-Tas, who does respond to the calls of men and women who pursue the light of freedom yet do not know of the violet flame. Hail unto the children of light! Hail to the elementals! For they are invited also to enter into the Cathedral of the Violet Flame to be saturated with that light, to be cleared of all of the burdens of the planes of mankind's consciousness."

Violet-flame clearance of the soul chakra and cleansing of the West Coast. On October 9, 1976, Omri-Tas came for the clearing of the soul chakra of Terra, of America and of every soul on earth. Dictating in Pasadena, California, he announced: "We would cleanse this coast of the records of infamy and rebellion, of hatred of the Mother and selfishness of her children. . . . We are starting a violet flame action here in the heart of the City of the Angels and here in the heart of the Mother and the devotees that will go around the circle of fire, around the entire border of Lemuria, consuming, consuming with the all-powerful light of the violet transmuting flame the records of misuse of the light of love in God-obedience. . . . Now I raise my arms for the release of sacred fire into the depths of the Pacific at that point where the seven Holy Kumaras released the flame of Mother and the rising action. So we penetrate to the ocean floors of the planet the release of the violet flame for the rebalancing of energies and conditions in earth, in water, in air and throughout the etheric plane."

Inauguration of the Aquarian age. Alpha cycle of the violet flame. On December 29, 1976, Omri-Tas came with legions of violet-flame angels and priests and priestesses of the sacred fire for the inauguration of the Aquarian cycle "by the release of the violet flame from the very heart of the Violet Planet." In his dictation, given in Pasadena, Omri-Tas said: "We come to take up residence on Terra for the age of Aquarius and for the bringing in of that age. . . . We will make our abode in the residence of the Lord of the World . . . and we will stand with Terra until the turning of the cycles and the turning of the age. . . . Angels of the Violet Planet and priestesses of the sacred fire together with the mighty hosts, the 144,000 priests who yet hold the focus in the heart of the Violet Planet, have begun that ritual of saturating the earth plane with the action of the violet flame that is for the purpose of the transmutation of millions of years of the qualification of energy on Terra. . . . We come, then, to introduce the age of ritual, of science and of alchemy."

Omri-Tas also gave the following promise: "From the point of Alpha at Shamballa I will stand to release my light into the heart of the Mother, into the hearts of all who would be Mother, into the hearts of all Keepers of the Flame. And each morning with the first ray of the dawn that caresses the face and the heart of the devotee, I will send forth the electric spark, the current of the Alpha cycle of the violet flame. And in that moment you may catch that spark and be and receive the Omega return and therefore be unto me throughout the twenty-four-hour cycle the Omega counterpart of the Alpha-concentrated energies, which I place now upon the altar of Shamballa, adding unto the mighty threefold unfed flame of Sanat Kumara, of Gautama Buddha, of Lord Maitreya a magnificent outpouring of violet light, which now ensconces the threefold flame as a basin, a lotus basin of light. . . . The focus that is placed at Shamballa will also be transferred by the thread of contact of the Lord of the World, reinforced by the legions of violet-flame angels in every heart that lives and breathes and has life because the Lord of the World does keep that flame of life for the evolutions of Terra." (1977 *Pearls of Wisdom,* vol. 20, no. 14)

Multiplication of 15 minutes of violet flame. On July 6, 1984, in the Heart of the Inner Retreat, Omri-Tas announced the following dispensation for the multiplication of our decrees to the violet flame: "If in all reverence, with inner attunement, a sense of yourself in your Christ Self as priest or priestess of the sacred fire, if with all your heart and deep within your heart you will take, then, fifteen minutes each day to give *profound* and loving invocations to the violet flame in my name (and please remember to use my name, for I am the one from whose causal body this dispensation comes), then we will take that offering, measure for measure as it is devoted, as it is profound and sincere, the very weight of its power and light. Therefore, by the *quality* of it, quality for quality, it shall be multiplied in your life ten times!" (1984 *Pearls of Wisdom,* vol. 27, no. 50A)

Violet-flame reservoir over central Europe. On February 26, 1988, in a dictation given in Lisbon, Portugal, Omri-Tas announced the dispensation of a violet-flame reservoir positioned over central Europe: "It is a very large reservoir of light as a sea in itself; and this light, beloved, is there for you to invoke as a direct transfusion to all lightbearers of Europe, Eastern Europe and the entire Soviet bloc. . . . When you invoke the violet flame, it will draw forth the light of this reservoir and also maximize it, fortify it, multiply it by your own love and devotion; and therefore that light shall flow to every lightbearer in these lands. And as it does flow to them it shall quicken them, it shall cut them free, it shall therefore transmute their spiritual and physical blindness as to those events coming. . . . This reservoir is a certain dispensation. If those Keepers of the Flame in embodiment do not make the violet-flame call daily, then this reservoir will come to be used up in its entirety, apportioned then among all lightbearers. But if the call continues to be given, the reservoir shall be like the unfed flame. It shall not fail. It shall remain full and all that goes out of it shall be returned unto it multiplied by your call." (1988 *Pearls of Wisdom,* vol. 31, no. 33)

Violet-flame sea of light. On May 1, 1991, in Portland, Oregon, Omri-Tas announced the unprecedented dispensation of the violet-flame sea of light: "I deposit in the heart of the earth a dispensation immense of concentrated violet flame. It is an intercession of the quality of mercy. It is an intercession afforded to all those who serve the light. And through your Holy Christ Self it shall be meted out as an unguent, as an elixir. May you drink of it in your hours of need and in your hours of strength and keep it replenished by new calls to the violet flame. It is a giant violet-flame reservoir, as a sea of light pulsating." (1991 *Pearls of Wisdom,* vol. 34, no. 26)

Omri-Tas to be present on earth on the third of each month. On October 14, 1991, Omri-Tas announced a thirty-three-day dispensation in which he would remain on earth to "give us a boost" and multiply our violet-flame decrees. On November 16, 1991, at the conclusion of the thirty-three days, Omri-Tas granted another tremendous dispensation. The messenger and chelas had written petitions to Omri-Tas, asking him to remain longer and offering pledges of violet-flame decrees. In response, Omri-Tas said that he was profoundly moved by our offering but that he could not remain on earth full-time. He said there were many other planets at a similar crossroads to that of earth who were in great need of his presence. However, he was so touched by the Keepers of the Flame's pledges of daily violet-flame decrees that he promised to return to earth once a month on the third day of the month for twenty-four hours. The messenger has declared the third of each month to be Omri-Tas' Violet Flame Day and urges Keepers of the Flame to hold violet-flame vigils in their sanctuaries from midnight to midnight. She recommends that we prepare for the coming of Omri-Tas by dedicating the second day of the month to building a rolling momentum of blue decrees, so that the legions of the first ray of all of cosmos can clear the way for a greater penetration of the violet flame on the third. From the moment the midnight hour strikes, beginning Omri-Tas' Violet Flame Day, there will be groups of Keepers giving the violet flame. Because there are Keepers of the Flame throughout the world in every time belt, the entire twenty-four hours will be covered.

Those who desire to do a two-day vigil would begin on the second of the month, giving calls to Archangel Michael, the Archangel Michael Rosary, decrees to Surya and Astrea and any or all of the decrees in the blue section of the decree book, as well as Reverse-the-Tides and Judgment Calls. For those who can only give a one-day vigil, the most important day is the third of the month. As the messenger has said, "That is the day when walls of violet flame can come down and we can be directly in the Electronic Presence of Omri-Tas." For those who prefer to do some of their vigil on the first day and some on the second day, the messenger recommends a minimum of two hours of blue decrees on the second of the month and two hours of violet-flame decrees on the third. In preparation for Omri-Tas' Violet Flame Day each month, Keepers may wish to fast and pray. The messenger recommends fasting on pressure-cooked brown rice (it may be toasted before being pressure-cooked) and bancha tea (also known as kukicha, or twig, tea). It is permissible to do this fast for three days. Rice should be considered as a sacred food and chewed no less than fifty times per mouthful. It is good to eat it slowly, taking sips of bancha tea. The messenger has said that if the Keepers are able to fast and make the violet-flame day the third day of their fast, this will increase even further the dispensation of Omri-Tas.

CHAPTER 11

Jesus Christ

THE CALL OF LOVE

In Preparation for the Wedding Day

Your Marriage to Jesus Christ

My beloved brides, I receive you to my heart in preparation for the wedding day. I come to you as you have come to me. And in this hour love suffuses our hearts as my Sacred Heart enfolds your own. And in this moment in the bridal chamber we prepare your soul for the entering in, which shall surely take place as you weave and continue to weave your wedding garment. Gifts of the violet flame given to you are also for the weaving of this garment. It is called the deathless solar body.

And you also recall the parable where the one came in to the marriage feast having not the wedding garment and that one was cast into outer darkness.[1] For, you see, your wedding must take place in the etheric octave, and to be in that octave you must have the appropriate soul apparel—the wedding gown and the bridal veil.

These garments, beloved, are the garments you are to perfect. For as you have been told, there are rents in your garment caused by all manner of intrusions, tears that come from encounters on the astral plane or the violent misuse of the light, from the rhythms of Antichrist and all manner of attacks upon your soul.

I, Jesus, desire to assist you in your preparations, for the wedding date is set and I, your Lord, expect you to be in that secret chamber at the appointed hour.

Indeed it is a boon—the gift of Omri-Tas, his presence and flame, of Saint Germain, the Maltese-cross formation and their multiplying of your calls to the violet flame by the violet-flame sea.[2] Surely you shall have the wisdom and the rejoicing in me to use this violet flame industriously so that the garment might be complete and strengthened and no more subject to the tears of the lower octaves.

It may be a bit difficult to visualize but nevertheless, beloved, you must call forth the armour of Archangel Michael and the seraphim of God, not only for the protection of your soul and your four lower bodies but also for the protection of this garment—the deathless solar body—as both the undergarment of humility and the outer garment of honor.

For is not honor born of humility?

For when one comes to comprehend the honor of God, is one not humbled before the great light, the dazzling white light of the presence of the cosmic honor flame?

Honor, then, is an homage that you pay unto the living Christ that I AM and unto your God. It is the honoring of the light that is unsullied and untainted, the light that is the strength that holds together the Matter cosmos.

Honor is a strength beyond other strengths. Honor is purity. Honor is the majesty of God. It is the single-eyed vision and the adoration of the one true God. Honor is oneness. It is wholeness.

One cannot enter into its precincts without the ultimate understanding of humility, for humility is before God and before the living flame. It is a self-effacement for a purpose: that the lesser self be sealed and the Greater Self appear. It comes down to the saying I gave to your Catherine, "I the All: thou the nothing—I the All: thou the nothing."[3]

Thus, as you say it unto me, you say, "O Jesus, my Lord, thou the All and I the nothing. Thou the All and I the nothing!" And as you say it, beloved, my Christ Presence becomes my allness in you, and the mortal self disintegrates and the True Self is manifest. It is a yin and yang action of Alpha and Omega.

O Jesus, my Lord, thou the All of me: I the nothing. Take my nothingness, O my Lord, and let me be the allness of thyself. Be the Christ in me, my Lord, and I shall be worthy—worthy to be thy bride, as thou art the Lamb and thou art worthy before the throne of God.

So it is, beloved, the transformation of self by the displacement-replacement. The honor of God it is.

In the sanctuary of love I commune with your heart—first with the heart, beloved. Now feel my Sacred Heart, for I desire you to probe with me the elements of heart that require healing, transmutation.

I give you to see now fractures in the mandala of the heart, violations of the twelve petals of the heart. I allow you to see the imbalance of the threefold flame and records of the past that show you clearly how in choices made you have reduced rather than increased that flame. I show you this in love, beloved, for love imparts truth and vision.

Having the vision now, as I show it to you, of your Holy Christ Self, you can see how much you are mirroring of that Self and how you can mirror more by meditating on the elements of the Christ Self and Christ flame that are wanting in the mirror of self.

I hold you, beloved, I strengthen you as you look and see. Let it be an objective and scientific study of who and what you are today and all that you can be tomorrow.

O my Holy Christ Self—thou the All and I the nothing—be thou myself as Holy Christ flame burning on the altar of my heart for my Jesus, my Bridegroom, my Lord!

Sweetness is indeed the taste of the living Christ flame. Taste, then, the essence of myself. Know it is the portion also of your Holy Christ Self.

Thus know me as your sweet Jesus but know me also as your counsellor, confessor, and chastiser. I also come for the taming of the shrew of the lesser self, called the wretch.

Yes, beloved, this is a shadow, a shriveled-up form, a garment no longer worn but yet remaining in your closet. I strengthen you to take it out and see it. See this part of the not-self, the not-so-nice part of you. You take it. I hand it to you now and bid you cast it into the violet flame.

Be done with it! And see how the flame rejoices to consume it!

Oh, what gifts of wonder of the violet flame I did impart to my disciples and others of you in various ages, as you have been in the violet-flame temples of Atlantis! No wonder you are so happy to give the violet-flame decrees in this embodiment! You have longed for the violet flame, thirsted for it, sought it in the drinking of Communion's wine and the partaking of the bread. You have waited for the dispensation to come to you again and it has come, and you have become the devotees of the seventh ray.

May you also become brides of the seventh-ray hierarch, Saint Germain. May you become brides of the Holy Spirit, as Mother Mary did become the bride of the Holy Spirit.

Yes, beloved, when all of chaos and Old Night[4] and Armageddon threaten without like a violent winter storm, is it not good to commune in the secret chamber of the heart and to know a compartment of eternity that shall one day be the vastness of interstellar space for thee and me alone and for thee and thy twin flame?

Seek the marriage to the Christ! All other things shall come to you. Seek the Sacred Heart! Seek my Blood and my Body. Seek me everywhere!

Each time you find a corner of self where the rays of light now penetrate and you find the skeletons in your closet, so visualize my face and body, my presence there.

Remember the initiations I underwent in my final incarnation that you might know the pattern, the preparation of the soul through the violet flame for her own initiations: the forgiveness of the waters of the human consciousness as they become the wine, the sanctification of marriage as a sacrament in the Church and as the wedding of the soul to her Lord. Remember the path and the initiation of the alchemy of supply and the multiplication of the loaves and fishes by the power of Alpha and Omega.

Remember all of these footsteps while you are yet able to balance heart, head, and hand by violet flame. For this is the goal and the mandate of your soul's physical incarnation. Remember the point of entering into congruency with the perfection of your inner blueprint by that divine direction.

Remember, then, the transfiguration as the soul enters into and receives the impression of the perfect pattern of her Holy Christ Self to be outpictured. Remember the crucifixion, for Christ in thee must yet be crucified. Yes, remember living in the heart of the earth in the presence of resurrection's flame as I did. Remember the resurrection. Remember the forty days of profound inner temple instruction following. Remember the ascension.

These are the key initiations and there are many in between. Resist them not, resist me not! Resist not my footprints in the sands! Resist me not, beloved.

And surely know the confession of the soul and the holy sacrament of penance. Know the baptism. Know the Communion. Know that thou canst be a part of holy orders and yet maintain the rites of marriage and family in the holiness of God. Remember the soul's appearing with first breath and the soul's departure with the last.

The consecration of these rituals, beloved, becomes a part of the larger spiral that is your soul's bonding to my Sacred Heart and is there as matrix complete when you are received as my bride and the bride of the Christ of you.

This moment of the fusion of hearts is a moment that comes after the final exams, as it were, of your life's record, your going out of the way and coming in again, going out of the way and coming in again, until finally all desire to go out is purged from you and your sole and principal desire is to remain bonded to my heart and never, never again to violate that sacred vow of our union. For this calling I did descend to rescue your soul, who had broken the tie to my heart.

I am come, beloved. Do not tarry and tarry again in the outer way unto future ages down the halls of eternity. Take the initiation in this hour. Oh, take it! Take it and work so much good by my Sacred Heart [that has] become thy heart.

Surely this is the key to your becoming a candidate for the ascension. Surely thou canst not ascend without the prior bonding to that heart. Know it early, that all the days of thy life thou might impart to many the flame of love that is the bonding of our union.

I woo you to the bridal chamber that you might bear in your being and life that special love that all recognize and know as my love. When you are bonded to my heart you also have the Holy Spirit, whose gifts you can increase and multiply.

I desire you to be, as it were, salesmen for God,[5] for the path of Christic union, for love itself. The world has not tasted the sweetness of this love, and souls who have lost it so long ago cannot remember the taste.

Let them know it through you, beloved! Let them know it! Let them know a love that rekindles a desire within them to also go and get that love, to seek me and find me even when I play hide-and-seek with them to test their real desiring to see if they will be deterred by an easier search and the finding of some lesser manifestation.

Inspire them to seek true love, the true love of Christ. Inspire them by your joy and patience, your meekness, as well as the emboldening power of Elohim upon you taking wise dominion over the territories of the earth body in the sense of the territories of the mind and the heart and the domains of consciousness as compartments of being.

Yes, beloved, let my love in you be the irresistible force of cosmos that draws souls who can be drawn in by no other way but by my love. For having been beaten and bruised in so many circumstances, having had their loves betrayed again and again, these need the comfort of my love in you.

I the All of love within you: thou the All of love in me. Let this be the magnet of the Central Sun and your offering of gratitude upon the altar of God that you might now know and be and enter the golden cycle of the sun!

Oh, such a precious meeting of hearts in this place has come about! May you, as a nucleus of lightbearers worldwide, become the mandala of my Sacred Heart—the pattern, the form, the oneness, the heart of the mystical body.

Oh, know this love tryst, beloved, and hasten to the altar of the marriage of thy soul to Christ!

This is my voice in which I speak to you, this is my message as I speak in the tenderness of the Divine Mother and the quietness of the Father, who does oversee the preparations of your soul.

I am your Jesus if you will have me. And if you will, I counsel you, drink, drink, drink quickly the elixir of violet flame for the dispelling of forgetfulness, for the remembering of all that we have been together since the beginning of our going forth from the Central Sun.

I call to all of those who have been a part of myself and my life. I call them through you and I call directly to their hearts. I *call* and I *call* and I *call* again! It is the call of love.

May the many who have not received me who once knew me be reached by your outreaching of your heart, your hand, and your speaking of my truth.

Thou dost know and have my truth, beloved. Truth is an activating force of the Holy Spirit in your life. Let it take you where it will take you and move you as it will move you! Let it speak through you or be silent. Let it testify of me.

I am the witness of the God of love. May you be the witness of my flame, offering salvation by a path of rigorous discipleship in the rituals of love unfolding and becoming love.

O Holy Spirit, O the allness of God, descend upon each one according as the Holy Ghost is wont!

I, Jesus, stand in the temple of the Central Sun even as I am here. And I establish, therefore, an arcing of light to your being that you might see and glimpse and remember the great cathedral that is called the Temple Beautiful. I assure you, beloved, that on your wedding day you shall be beautiful in the Temple Beautiful.

I seal your vows and send you back to life's journey with all of the zeal of the love we share forever and forever and forever.

Amen! [Audience replies, "Amen."]

October 14, 1991
New Orleans, Louisiana

CHAPTER 12

Archangel Michael

NEW BEGINNINGS

The Protection of the Divine Plan of The Summit Lighthouse

I, Michael, Prince of the Archangels, do stand in the center of the Sun and in the center of the causal body of this messenger, which is now upon her. Therefore I am in the heart of the Central Sun, I am here below, and I establish new beginnings and new foundations built upon the old, yet strengthened by and strengthening the old unto the fullness of the New Day appearing!

I AM Michael! And I have set forth a cosmos of divine protection for this Summit Lighthouse in the beginning and I shall sustain it unto the ending of the cycles of its purpose in the Matter cosmos.

Yes, beloved, I have sent forth the ray with my sword of blue flame for the protection of the divine plan in this activity. And *you* are that divine plan, for the divine plan is fulfilled through your causal body of light.

On August 7, 1958, the ascended master El Morya founded The Summit Lighthouse through the messenger Mark L. Prophet. On that day the messenger Mark L. Prophet, Frances K. Ekey, and Christel F. Anderson gathered in Philadelphia for the first board meeting. Seven ascended masters—Archangel Michael, Elohim Peace, Saint Germain, the Maha Chohan, El Morya, Gautama Buddha, and Godfre—delivered dictations, releasing the original dispensations for The Summit Lighthouse. On August 11, 1991, these seven "founding fathers" returned again to dictate through the messenger Elizabeth Clare Prophet and to deliver their dispensations for the thirty-third anniversary.

Therefore be ye bodhisattvas on the path of the first ray of your dear El Morya and myself and so many others who bring to you not alone the power of the will of God but the fullness of that power of the will of God in manifestation.

There is no commodity such as pure power, beloved! Power that is true, that is of God, is always qualified by the will of God, by the mind of God, by the love of God, and by the law of the Divine Mother, as Above, so below.

Therefore let your own Dharmakaya descend upon your form and soul and heart! And when I say "let," beloved, I say pick up your shovels and shovel away the debris that blocks that manifestation upon you that you see now upon your messenger! That Dharmakaya of the I AM THAT I AM cannot fully integrate with the person here below until that person accomplish certain requirements of the Great Law.

Therefore, *you*—building in new beginnings in your individual world, beginning with this cycle of the anniversary of the thirty-three—must build those foundations whereby you can receive that holy light. And it is not out of the question that you can also have that attainment. Yet the 100 percent balancing of your karma must be your goal. Yet the integration with your Holy Christ Self and the mighty heart of Jesus Christ must be your goal and your accomplishment, beloved, as well as the flow of love unceasing that comes only from the point of God-harmony in the balanced threefold flame.

Yes, beloved, you may look for the star of your Presence and you may know that that star does draw nigh to you and that your goal of union with God must not be postponed unto the day of your ascension!

Did not Elijah walk in the fullness of the I AM THAT I AM and did not the great one of old, Elisha? And did not they who came from the Far East?

Indeed they did. They were the true mighty ones of old and unto them the Nephilim could not hold a candle.

Yes, beloved, in times past there have been those in the earth who did walk in the fullness of the God Presence. Now let it be the goal of those of you who have thirty-three years yet left in this life and much more.

For some of those whom I reach with my ray and presence are babes in arm or yet in the womb. And they shall come forth and achieve a life span whereby, if you will care for them properly, they may actually manifest the power of the three-times-thirty-three, yes, the three-times-thirty-three unto the ninety-nine.

Care for them well and build solid foundations in each of the four lower bodies and you shall see what God shall work through you and what he has already wrought through you as you have dedicated yourselves to bring forth these children, aye, children and more—sons of God, I say, and Christed ones.

Therefore spare not the rod and spare not yourselves the trouble of working and loving and teaching these children. For you will understand that they shall carry the torch you pass to them when the days come that you are feeble in the body and more of your spirit is ascending and you are winding those coils of fire unto that victory of translation, even as Enoch was translated unto the octaves of light.[1]

Therefore I say, beloved, let the conclusion of this year and cycle of the celebration of the thirty-three be for the violet flame transmutation of all that should not have been within these thirty-three years and for the fulfillment of all that *should* be and should have been achieved.

Much has been achieved, beloved, and yet that measure and quality of the Christ consciousness that you have been called to embody has not been reached to the level that El Morya had hoped it would be. Yes, beloved, it is because you have allowed other desirings and the leaking of the energies of God in many directions. You have not seen how the disciplined ones and the bodhisattvas, in not one but many embodiments, have given their entire attention to the manifestation of this Christhood in imitation of the life of Jesus Christ—even the eighty-one years he lived in his final embodiment.[2]

Yes, beloved, *The Imitation of Christ*[3] is yet the book that you must keep at bedside and read, even a page each night, imitating the ways of Christ until your imitation is become the divine Reality *unmoved,* and I say unmoved, beloved!

A personal, individual Christhood is the challenge of the number thirty-three. How many of you have advanced to that age in this audience this day?

Those of you who have attained to thirty-three and beyond, you see, are expected, increment by increment, to exude that Christ flame. Some of you who have not yet reached that age, even some little ones, have more of that Christhood than those who have gone beyond. Yet age in physical years is not the determining factor but the foundations laid in previous incarnations and the awareness, beloved.

Therefore, I *pierce* by my sword of blue flame—yes, the same sword that I raised up over that city of Philadelphia, that City of Brotherly Love, where the love ray went forth for the founding of this activity.* I take that same sword, beloved, and I pierce the density and the veils whereby you have not seen or been sensitized to the intimations of your I AM Presence, hence the intimations of the seven archangels, who stand before you this day!

May you kneel before the God flame within us, beloved ones, and recognize that we are that I AM THAT I AM fully in manifestation. Thus, you call us Lord Michael, Lord Jophiel, Lord Chamuel, Lord Gabriel, Lord Raphael, Lord Uriel, Lord Zadkiel.

We desire you to experience that wonder of God in us and the wonder of the archangelic hosts of light and all of their legions. We desire you to know that the same God that we are and have become is in you! And therefore, have reverence toward those who have gone beyond you who are that I AM in manifestation, that you might also have that reverence toward the flame in your heart, as tiny or as great as it may be, reverence in the sense that the holiness of the LORD your God is increasing daily.

---

*In his dictation on August 7, 1958, Archangel Michael said: "I am spreading over you the canopy of my love and my protection in the very beginning of this endeavor. The sword of blue flame is established in the upper atmosphere over the city of Philadelphia. . . . Do you realize, beloved, what a gracious opportunity this is in that you shall be a chalice of heaven into which I, Michael, shall charge the ray of protection for the God-plan made manifest in this which is to be the highest activity that I shall have sponsored since I took the first root race Home?"

If you have that sense of the holiness of your soul and spirit and mind and heart and temple, let holiness exude from you, beloved! Let it come forth from the pores of your skin, from your eyes and heart and chakras!

I charge you with the holiness flame of God to walk the earth from this day forward as a separate people who have that distinct vibration, who say in their heart:

"I AM holy, for the LORD my God is holy!"

[Congregation affirms with Archangel Michael:]

I AM holy, for the LORD my God is holy!
I AM holy, for the LORD my God is holy!
I AM holy, for the LORD my God is holy!

Therefore do not convey to the little ones or to the new students a certain secularism regarding the teachings of the ascended masters. There is not a secular vibration in our teaching, beloved. Every word we speak and that is spoken by the messenger comes out of the Spirit cosmos and it has a sheath of holiness.

Do not be tempted to step down the teachings to an intellectual or an academic or an emotional format but have the holiness in your aura whereby you sweep up by that aura those in your audiences, those who come to hear the Word, and they are in the rapture of the holiness of God and therefore know the communication because it is transmitted to them through the messenger through you by the Holy Spirit. And only the word that is transferred by the Holy Spirit will work change in another! Know that, beloved.

Seek the quickening and know that the archangels are empowered to transfer to you a mighty light. And yet that presence of the Holy Spirit must be a point of enlightenment whom you obey.

Therefore listen, listen to the still small voice within.[4] Abide the promptings of your soul and your heart. Hearken unto your God and create the spaces of thinking, meditating, visualizing or simply stilling the mind, stilling the outer "things upon things" that come upon you, until you hear your God speaking to you of your mission, of your love that is God's and of those things to which you must pay attention in order to have your victory on the morrow and on the next day and on the next.

Are your knees troubling you, beloved?*

Yes, understand the saints who have knelt hour upon hour, year upon year and even in the etheric retreats of the Brotherhood doing their penance. For they have seen what they did not fulfill on earth and therefore a mighty penance did they put upon themselves in order to reincarnate and be able to bring with them the holiness of God and that divine love—these two qualities which they did fail to develop in their previous lives.

Come now, beloved ones. Understand that you must examine your day's preoccupations of the mind and the body and the feelings and the memory. And take command, I say! *Take command* in the name of the seven archangels of *your life* and *your will* and *your love* and the application of knowledge and wisdom given unto you!

Yes, beloved, seek adeptship! It has been said. I say it again: Seek adeptship. Above all, do not make the single mistake of being satisfied with yourself as you are today. And I shall tell you a secret of the seven archangels: We are not satisfied as we manifest God today, and on the morrow you shall see seven archangels in a new manifestation! We are never the same, beloved, but always incorporating, embodying in our great bodies of light more of the God who is the Limitless One.

Yes, beloved. Never rest upon your oars and remain satisfied! If you will obey my command to you this day and that of the other six who stand with me in agreement—to seek adeptship—you shall build another thirty-three-year spiral and see how this Lighthouse shall cover the earth with the light of love and draw all men and women and children to their mighty I AM Presence and to the mighty lineage of Sanat Kumara, Gautama Buddha, Lord Maitreya, Jesus Christ, and Padma Sambhava.

Thus, beloved, be humbled before your God and be emboldened before the world! Know the difference and recognize that there is a penance to be paid by every one of you for the misuse of the sacred fire under the hierarchy of Capricorn—that is, the misuse of power.

*The congregation has been kneeling as Archangel Michael instructed.

Therefore know that the knees relate to Capricorn,[5] and on your knees you feel the pain of past abuses of God's power even as you pray to God in this moment for the transmutation of your misuses of that light.

Therefore as we attend you, we give you these moments to pray aloud to your God that you might have the clearing of the crown chakra and the twelve o'clock line as you go forth to fling a new spiral for this activity of light! Let us hear the prayer of the holy who do the will of God as love!

[Congregation offers invocations and prayers to God.]

I bid you rise into a new awareness of self in the holiness of God, the love of God, the light of God, and the will of God, which compute as God-power.

You need the power of God, beloved. We have that power and we desire to convey it to you. Therefore the messenger has taught that to sing to us as you begin your service or your lectures is the key to unlock the power of cosmos of the seven rays through our Electronic Presence.

We guarantee that we place our Electronic Presence over you whenever our song is sung, and that we give protection to those who come in to hear the Word. And we protect them, in answer to your calls, from those who would tear them from the breast of the Divine Mother even before they can drink her milk and be weaned to be strengthened on their own.

Yes, beloved, as far as I am concerned, I can only express gratitude to you for producing and using the tapes you have dedicated to me—the rosary and the songs and decrees.[6] Yes, beloved, thanks to you, my name has been heard throughout the earth, and I have stamped my electronic vibration upon every erg of energy and grain of sand of this planet.

I shall increase it and I shall continue to be the absolute God-protection of you and this messenger and the entire family of light-bearers who make up the pillar of fire in the earth that is The Summit Lighthouse. Yes, beloved, may you continue to call to me, for I am authorized this day to continue that protection by which there did go forth the initial sponsorship of this activity.

I AM Michael! I stand in the heart of the Sun. I stand in the heart of your causal body and I AM Presence. May you pull me down and make me comfortable *where you are.*

I love you in the name of God. I love you in the name of God.

[35-second standing ovation]

August 11, 1991
Royal Teton Ranch,
Park County, Montana

CHAPTER 13

Elohim Peace

I INAUGURATE A THIRTY-THREE-TIERED SPIRAL OF PEACE IN THE SUMMIT LIGHTHOUSE

Keep the Flame of Cosmic Christ Peace!

Peace, be still and know that I AM Elohim Peace! And where I AM there is the peace of Aloha. I AM THAT I AM peace in you. And I am called of God from the beginning unto the ending in the cycles of this activity to establish the Cosmic Christ flame of peace!

And in my original dictation, beloved, I did release a prayer for peace that I did ask the students to offer. May this prayer be yours. May you use it daily. And may you visualize a large, fiery, blazing sun at the solar plexus, the "place of the sun," the place where Cosmic Christ peace must be established in you.

Shaft of golden light and purple, flecked in ruby, descending upon you now is for the alignment of chakras and the healing of your physical organs and their etheric counterparts. Be seated in my shaft of peace, beloved.

Peace, be still and know that the I AM that is God in me is the God where you are! I AM Alpha this day. You are my Omega counterpart. And, beloved, Aloha does place her Electronic Presence over you that you might know and enjoy the flame of God in the sixth ray. Therefore

I am come and therefore I have been given the mandate to keep the flame of peace in this activity.

I come as a cosmic teacher, beloved. I come to tell you that where there is not God-harmony there cannot be God-peace. Thus harmony is the other side of peace and peace the other side of harmony.

Know, then, the white fire. Know the central sun of being. Establish that sun. And do not allow yourselves to live upon the periphery of your auras, for there you shall be plucked by the fallen ones. But they cannot reach you when you are centered in the heart. And the heart of this activity—as the heart of God and the heart of El Morya and Lanello—the heart of this activity, beloved, in this octave must be your heart and all of your hearts as one.

Did not El Morya come forth to wrap the diamond heart of Mary in his own diamond heart, thus signifying the power of the masculine and the feminine ray, thus signifying the presence of the Cosmic Virgin in the founding of this community?

Aye, indeed, the blessed Mary has been a part of all those Sons of heaven who have nurtured this activity. Therefore know the "diamond heart within the diamond heart" and seek to have the twain envelop your own heart, beloveds. See your heart now enfolded in the heart of Mary, enfolded again in the heart of Morya. See the Trinity, then, of a Father- and a Mother-presence abounding round about you and your heart being strengthened by the matrix.

You must solve the chemistry of being here below and the biochemistry. You must know that you are made of points of light and atoms and cells and electrons. You are made of the substance of this octave, beloved. And I do not say "of the substance of earth" but I say "the substance of this octave," and I do not wish to be misquoted.

Therefore, because you are made of the substance of this octave, beloved, you must seek the divine harmony of the resonance of all atoms and cells in your being and all organs in your being with one another and with the etheric matrix and the etheric mandate. After all, we, Elohim of God, are builders of form. Builders of form are we! We must have, therefore, a chalice in every molecule of your body—your etheric, mental, desire, and physical bodies—in order to endow you with a greater light.

When you achieve the balance of harmony, beloved, then you can hold the greatest light. You have called this harmony the yang and the yin, the Alpha and the Omega, the plus and the minus, and it is so. When you find that equilibrium at each level of your being, beloved, and become alchemists of your own temple, you shall see how much more of God you can hold within those vessels of chakras, organs, and all the components of being.

Yes, beloved, I AM Peace. Where there is the warring in the members, where there is the teetering and tottering of the imbalance from day to day between the emotions and the thoughts, where there is not strength and fire raised up as the *virya*[1] of the Buddha in you, how can we add unto you increments of fire when the fire would only make matters worse?

In the extreme, beloved, there are the deranged and the insane and those who have made their pact with darkness and therefore erupt as volcanoes with anger and all sorts of blasphemy speaking through them. They may not come near the altar of God. They must go forth and balance themselves, for they are in rebellion against the law of God at every level of being.

There is a chemistry for the mind, another for the desire body, and another for the etheric body. When you attain that balance, you will find the Path to be one of peace. Attain peace in your members, beloved. And you know whereof I speak! Thus, I shall not warn again lest you have the karma of neglecting the warning of hierarchy. We leave it, then, to the messenger and other representatives of the Path to speak to you concerning these things.

I say, then, beloved, to seek out harmony in all that you are, you must invoke the violet flame for the transmutation of layers of misqualified substances and karmic records. How can you attain God-harmony with the records of a past karma that trouble you at the deepest levels of being?

Thus, there must be surrender to your God to have peace. There must be the all-desiring of God to have peace. Did not the great one of peace, Gautama, teach you that inordinate desiring is suffering and that this is the cause of suffering?

If you suffer, then, on a daily basis, warring in your mind and body and being burdened by those conditions, I give you opportunity this day. For this day I, the Elohim of Peace, unleash a new cycle, a spiral of peace within this activity, and I inaugurate that spiral of peace for each one of you, beginning beneath the feet and going up as high as your causal body of light. It is a thirty-three-tiered spiral of peace, if you will.

Yes, beloved, you can mount that spiral and you can stay on each tier until you have achieved peace in that tier.

Yes, beloved, I say, this is the day when the heavens have opened, when the causal body of both of your messengers has opened. This is the day when you can say:

The Path of the Elohim of Peace

> Enough! I have had done with my human creation and I choose to enter the path of the Elohim of Peace! I choose to now receive the original endowment of peace that Elohim Peace gave upon the founding of this organization.
>
> I shall become that point of peace to which every angel ministering on earth shall have recourse. Yes, in my heart the flame of peace shall abide. Therefore I shall be unmoved. I shall not be moved by what does transpire *anywhere* outside the circle of my being or within it.
>
> This day I have said: Enough is enough! I am the victim of my own wrong desiring. I am the victim of my abuse of my four lower bodies. I am the victim of my karma. And this day I say, I shall no longer be the victim of myself but I shall be the instrument of God!
>
> I shall walk out from this court of King Arthur and I shall keep my vow to keep my counsel, keep my peace, keep the sealing of my words and to control the flashing forth of dark thought or feeling and the revolving of negative spirals of the memory.

I can do all of this, for I am the child of the heart of El Morya, my beloved. I can do all of this because my God is with me. I have a path, I have Maitreya, I have a messenger whom I can see and touch and who will love me and comfort me and help me and rebuke me and lead me.

Yes, I am in the best possible position that my karma allows me to be in. For I know there is no injustice anywhere in the universe and I am truly convinced that there is mercy beyond mercy that I have this opportunity this day to remake myself by the power of Elohim in the image and likeness of Almighty God, by the power of the Word with Brahman in the Beginning.

Yes, I will work with Elohim of Peace. And I know that because God sent Elohim to endow this activity that this activity is sponsored from the Elohimic level and all the power of Elohim is upon me and the mighty chalice of the resurrection flame in the Heart of the Inner Retreat.[2]

Yes, I shall take the dispensations of Elohim, for they are power in the seven rays. They are the power of Alpha and Omega. And I shall remake myself that I might carry the spiral of the next thirty-three years of this activity until The Summit Lighthouse transcends the octaves here below as Above and its beams shed their powerful light into the depths of death and hell so that souls caught in those levels may follow the beam to the heart of their I AM Presence and receive the archangels' deliverance.

Yes, I will walk in the living flame of peace. I shall be a true pilgrim of peace. And I shall show the two-edged sword dividing the Real from the unreal, binding the engines and elements of war.

Yes, I know the meaning of true peace and I know it is not pacifism. I know that the power of peace will swallow up the records of war upon this planet as I take the mantra:

Peace, be still and know that I AM God!
Peace, be still and know that I AM God!
Peace, be still and know that I AM God!

[Congregation joins Elohim Peace:]

Peace, be still and know that I AM God!

May you say it with the fire with which I have given it! I speak to all who come to study—those who would be ministering servants, those who would be chelas and disciples, those who would pursue their professions now at hand—and I say to you, beloved: Learn to release the fire of the heart, the sacred fire, and to be infilled again and learn it with this mantra. Hear how it is spoken:

"Peace, be still and know that I AM God!"

Blessed ones, it is not mere volume but it is the power of the sacred fire released in the volume:

"Peace, be still and know that I AM God!"

Thus the fire goes forth, beloved, and the power is released. May you practice. May you feel the light raised up in the chakras by your mantras and meditations, by your devotions. And may you learn that the most powerful fiat and decree you can utter is the one that you endow with the sacred fire.

Learn of me. Learn of your messengers. And understand that some defy the power of God and will not speak forth when called upon to do so! They consider it beneath them to raise their voices, to let the Lord's power flow through them.

It is a defiance of God, beloved, to refuse to raise the voice above a common conversational tone and it is also a defiance of God to raise the voice in anger or at any time you are not in control of your thoughts, feelings, acts or unconscious momentums. Therefore be in God-control and know when is the moment to let the volume rise to reach a heart enslaved, a heart and a soul and a body infested with demons. For that one cannot hear you unless the fire go forth to strip from him that which does assail him!

Be ashamed, then, to be called a minister of God if you refuse to master the spoken Word and the delivery of the fohat. You will have it when you let the sacred fire of the Mother rise within you. Let it be at first an imitation in the privacy of your own room or as you walk alone in the hills. Yes, beloved, it does take practice and it does take the call to Elohim and archangels and the Maha Chohan. But the fire of the spoken Word must go forth!

As far as we are concerned, the individual prophet, messenger, apostle is defined by the level of fire that is in him or her, and none can attain to that calling unless ordained by God. Thus, you who would become the lay servant, the ministering servant, beloved, must know it is a step in the right direction, and yet the power of God must go forth from you in time of need. And you cannot rise to another level of appointment until you achieve some measure of the power of God by obedience to his will, by surrender and sacrifice and selflessness in service.

Yes, beloved, you see, until you have this power, it is dangerous for you to have the next and the next mantle. Therefore make your peace with the power of God that is his will and know that peace is God-harmony, peace is God-control and peace is God-reality!

I could speak on of power and I shall for a moment, but I shall also leave to the meditation of your heart the proving of the necessity for the establishment of the blue-flame cross in your world.[3] And when you make that sign of the cross nine times,[4] think in your heart: *"I AM God-power, God-harmony, God-reality, God-control.* This is my blue-flame cross and I reject all misqualifications of that blue-flame cross in my world!" For these misqualifications are the stumbling block to Christhood and the nonfulfillment of some devotees.

Yes, beloved, power must become something in the hand and the heart, something in the throat chakra, something in the mind that is there as a resource, that when you encounter Evil that light flashes forth from you because it is of God and not because you force it and not because you enter into the reactionary human consciousness.

Yes, beloved, be at peace in the centeredness of God-power, in our definition of the word, in the four quadrants of the cardinal signs.

Yes, beloved, be at the center of peace so that when there is danger and challenge of your office, God shall release the power through you, whether you speak in the still small voice of fire or in the resounding power of that fire.

Comprehend my meaning, beloved, for the cycles become physical and the challenges so. We, Elohim, come to your aid. We, Elohim, say: Come to our level and know the ultimate protection and the ultimate chelaship.

I AM Peace. I AM the peace-commanding presence of the Cosmic Christ. I AM the peace-commanding presence of Almighty God. Therefore, I command you: *Peace, be still and know that the I AM in you is God!* Be ashamed to violate that peace.

And now I charge every one of you, from the least unto the greatest, as you perceive yourselves: You must receive the gentle rebuke from anyone of this community when you abandon your point of peace. Let every brother and sister remind one another, regardless of rank or position or background or standing, that where there is the breaking of harmony and the breaking of peace there is the fracturing of the mandala. Many tiny fractures in this mandala need healing.

Therefore do not react when someone in the still small voice of peace reminds you to return to your center, reminds you that whether in thought or feeling or word or vibration or in purpose or in plan, you have departed from peace. Take the reminder, beloved, and thank that one with all your heart. Call immediately upon the law of forgiveness. I ask you to become a fountain and a foundation of Cosmic Christ peace and thereby know our presence in your midst.

The byword of the peacemakers, beloved, is "I shall not be moved." Blessed are the peacemakers. Therefore affirm: In the name Jesus Christ, I shall not be moved!

Thus, the peacemaker must challenge the vibration of non-peace. But non-peace is not the power of God that resounds from the heart of peace and power.

Some think if another raise his voice, he is out of alignment. It is whether the raised voice is charged with anger and condemnation or whether it is charged with fire. And if there be a dispute, then let it be committed to the flame or referred to the messenger or the counsel of the board of directors.

Yes, beloved, disciples require the rebuke and those other disciples who rebuke them are not always perfect. Yet when they do counsel, let them first take a step back and say:

> Peace, be still and know that the I AM God in me is the I AM God in that one. And I go forth to establish Christ-peace, to teach a lesson, to correct an error. Therefore, O God, seal me in my tube of light, the violet flame, the mantle and the armour of God that I speak the word of truth and yet hold the God-harmony of peace.

Think what a magnet this shall be. It shall be the greatest antiwar manifestation on the face of planet Earth! This is my prediction and my prophecy! Will you make it come true?

["Yes!" (34-second standing ovation)]

I, Elohim Peace and Aloha, hold you to your word! The Law does hold you to your word and so does El Morya. Thus, I withdraw to the flame in your heart to assist you in keeping that flame of Cosmic Christ peace.

August 11, 1991
Royal Teton Ranch,
Park County, Montana

Pour Out the Radiant Golden Oil of Peace!

by the Elohim of Peace
August 7, 1958, Philadelphia

Beloved mighty Presence of God, which I AM in me, and beloved Elohim of Peace: from the zenith of the heavens pour out the radiant golden oil of peace unto the horizon of my world—to the 360 degrees of the circumference of my being that extends to the borders of time and eternity!

Fill the circle of my world and the worlds of all children of the light with such an effulgent light and love as is the manifest power of the Elohim of Peace that no dissonance or any other variant of peace can manifest where I AM—in the heart of Peace!

Beloved Elohim of Peace: From the zenith of the heavens, pour out the radiant golden oil of Peace unto the horizon of my world! (9x)

Elohim Peace and his divine complement, Aloha, are the Elohim of the sixth ray (the purple and gold ray) of peace, brotherhood, ministration and service. Elohim Peace and Aloha focus the gold and the purple flames as the perfect balance of the masculine and feminine aspects of peace. Their retreat is located in the etheric plane over the Hawaiian Islands, where they focus the energies of the solar-plexus chakra of the planet. From the Temple of Peace, they radiate ribbons of Cosmic Christ peace over the entire earth. Souls who are to embody on the sixth ray study for a time at the Temple of Peace in preparation for their mission. See *The Masters and Their Retreats,* pp. 281–84, 481–83.

Elohim is one of the Hebrew names of God, or of the gods; used 2,500 times in the Old Testament. It is a uni-plural noun that refers to the twin flames of the Godhead—the "Divine Us" who created male and female in their image and likeness. The Elohim embody the light of the Father-Mother God, whom they personify on each of the seven rays. These seven sets of twin God-flames are the "seven Spirits of God" referred to in Revelation 1:4; 3:1; 4:5; 5:6.

CHAPTER 14

Saint Germain

OUR MAGNET OF LOVE

The Pillar of Fire of Divine Love Descends upon This Altar: I Offer You the Cup of the Elixir of Divine Love

Hail, Keepers of the Flame of The Summit Lighthouse!

[Audience gives the salutation:]

Hail, Saint Germain! Hail, Saint Germain! Hail, Saint Germain!

[32-second standing ovation]

Hail, Christed ones who keep the flame of my fraternity! I am in your heart the living flame of cosmic freedom, and each time you invoke the flame of cosmic freedom as the living flame, I am there expanding the violet flame in your heart, which does bring about the balancing of that threefold flame and a multiplication factor that is beyond your reckoning.

Thus, beloved, to invoke the violet flame is to seal and secure the physical heart and the threefold flame. Thus I bid you enter my violet flame this day, for I come to serve. [5-second applause]

I come as servant—do I not?—to all the earth, to the heads of state, to the lowly and the heart that is humble. I have knocked on every door of every heart and home many a time in many a century, beloved. I am truly a beggar in many places. But here you have crowned me king and Portia queen of the age of Aquarius, thereby ratifying our assignment for the Aquarian age.

Is not, then, the spokesman for Christ Jesus also the beggar, beloved? And do you not go forth with your bowls sometimes filled offering the teaching itself? And as you open your mouth, they change the subject. And you wonder, is there not even a small curiosity as to what is the path of the mystics?

Well, I tell you, beloved, it is not a matter of curiosity; it is a question of heart. Where there is no heart flame akin to God's there is no desire for the Path or the teaching itself.

I therefore come to you that you might understand that you do walk in my footsteps. For I had many incarnations, as I had to confront the powerful of this world and many, many lifestreams. Consider yourself as a Keeper of the Flame walking in my footsteps and remember what Jesus said to his disciples: The servant is not greater than his lord. If they have persecuted me, they will persecute you also. If they have crucified me, they will crucify you also.[1]

But I, Saint Germain, am here to tell you this day that there does come an end to persecution and an end to the crucifixion, and I will tell you when that end does come. It does not come in the heart of the seed of the Wicked One, beloved. They are always there at a certain level of cosmic vibration below that of God. It comes, beloved, when *you* have made your peace with God, when *you* are wholly filled and wholly satisfied, when *you* are in the bliss of Lord Gautama Buddha and therefore do not even recognize persecution as persecution, for the fire of your being does consume it.

Visualize yourself now superimposed with the mighty presence of the Bodhisattva-Buddha Maitreya, flames rising about you, golden flames of light and enlightenment. You can truthfully say, beloved, that that world that considers itself to be the ultimate in the styles of reality is nothing but a chimera, nothing but maya and illusion. It is no part of your God-reality!

And it is up to *you* to maintain that bliss of God-reality, whether you descend to the thirty-third level of hell to preach to the fallen ones or ascend to the heights of the etheric octave or maintain the balance of both heaven and hell by determining to be in physical embodiment to hold the balance between them on behalf of those who cannot reach in either direction.

Yes, beloved, you do not need to languish, idling until the day when the kingdom of God shall come into manifestation! You need to be up and doing, working the works of God, building this mighty fire around you that is a conflagration that is felt by those whom you meet, that is an offense to the ungodly, and is the hearth of Home that the pilgrim of peace has been seeking round the world and back again all of his life.

Are you not the seeker?

Have you not found Maitreya?

Is it not time that you become Maitreya?

Ah yes! Yes, this is my prayer for you.

The Summit Lighthouse is the summation of cycles that you have not built but joined. The spiral of our beginnings in the holy seven, as Above, so below,* beloved, has been entered by you at that point in your life when you could catch the merry-go-round and get on and not be unbalanced.

Do you understand that the spin increases? Do you understand that the teaching becomes more pure, more simple, more complex and yet more obvious? Do you understand that you must be the step-down of the teaching?

You must embody the basic steps and have such clear footprints, such a clear sense of the geometry of God in your being that you can speak it with the clarity of a Clare or a Saint Francis, so clear to the listening ear—speaking to the inner child, speaking to the God of that one whom you address, speaking to the soul and heart and mind with

*The seven ascended founding fathers "Above," who gave the original dictations on August 7, 1958, and who dictated again on August 11, 1991; and the nucleus of the seven "below," comprised of the three who were present in Philadelphia for the founding of The Summit Lighthouse and the four who Archangel Michael promised would come to complete the seven. In 1961 Elizabeth Clare Prophet, then a student at Boston University, responded to the call of El Morya: "I have need of a feminine messenger. Go to Washington and I will train you through Mark Prophet." It was said that her arrival was the "squaring of the circle"—i.e., the original three became four, the number needed for the spiritual endowments to be anchored in the physical octave.

such a fervor that you will be either accepted or rejected immediately and you can continue to teach or move on, depending the response.

When you are lukewarm and the fires of your heart are not banked, you will get a lukewarm response. When you are on fire, there is no mistaking as to what that response will be. You see it continually in the case of the messenger and even yourselves.

It is best, beloved, aye, it is best to get it over with, to let the fire go forth—"let the chips fall where they may." For there are many to whom you must speak, many as you walk along life's way, and you ought to make the call each night to be taken out of your body during the sleep cycle to those in physical embodiment whom you cannot otherwise reach.

As you know, the old dispensation required the balancing of karma person-to-person ad infinitum, and thus the Hindu concept of thousands upon thousands of incarnations, beloved. Well, there is a point to that understanding. And if you desire to fulfill the whole law, you can do it out of the body. You can go forth while your body sleeps at night. This messenger goes forth and, whether at night or in the waking hours of the day, a portion of her being is always with us, working with the souls of humanity.

Therefore you can reach everyone and you will have the satisfaction of knowing the growth of your causal body, entering into cosmic heights once you shall have graduated from earth's schoolroom. And I trust not one of you is in a hurry to graduate, for we intend to leave you back in grades of former levels, beloved, to keep you here until the fulfilling of spirals. Do you mind, beloved? [Audience replies, "No!"]

We are grateful. For you are surely our bodies and our hands and our feet and we have much to do, much to do! And you can gain increments on your tree of life just as well here below, in fact better. For once you get the victory over that beast and are unmoved by yourself or another, why, I say, you will be that jolly good fellow! You will be that laughing Buddha. You will be unmoved and yet filled with the piercing fire that does quench the fiery darts of the wicked.[2] Never mind their fire! Just be certain that yours is greater.

Now, I did give the cup of liquid Light to my servants on the mountains of North America.[3] Yes, indeed, beloved. And I did pass the cup of Love to the founders of The Summit Lighthouse on that day and date of August 7, 1958.

Yes, beloved, and I come this day once again to offer the cup of Love. I have offered this cup to you at the Royal Teton Retreat[4] and I must say that you have not drunk all of it. You have sipped from it, beloved, and wisely so, for you have sipped but that amount that you could assimilate.

And the assimilation process of an elixir of Love is something to go through. It requires a path of initiation. The consequence of drinking too much of the elixir of Love ere you are ready for it is a certain poisoning of the system. And therefore, sip by sip you are able to drink and there are times scheduled at the Royal Teton Retreat for you to return again to drink another sip. This sip, beloved, affects the chakras and your being.

The more you prepare the physical body, the more that love is physical. The more you prepare the desire body, the more the desire body does vibrate with the desirings of divine love. The more you prepare the mind, the mental body, the more that body is endued with love. Thus, as you prepare the Omega manifestation, the Alpha may come to it and you may keep the Alpha in this octave in a bonding of Omega's light from my heart.

The etheric body, then, does absorb that essence even as you cleanse and clear it. Once again a note: This is the reason your Lanello has counseled you to clear the lines of the clock of the etheric quadrant and then the fire signs[5]—so that you might have pressing down from that memory body the image and likeness of God in which you are made and you may mirror it in the lower bodies.

Yes, beloved, all things are possible in God. Your predecessors in past golden ages, you yourselves who have lived in these ages have had stronger bodies than you do today (yet those bodies were not so embedded at these lower levels of density). Thus, because you have done so before, you can walk the earth again in this age empowered by love.

Is there any other power but love?

Love includes the love of the will of God, the love of harmony, the love of maintaining one's God-control in honor before Helios and Vesta and the love of reality that will not manufacture fantasy or phantoms or pure nonsense; nor will it allow the covering of the human by the speaking of untruths. Love, beloved, fulfills all lines of the clock when you understand it.

Oh yes, beloved, the foundation of this activity is love! Love brings to the blossoms in springtime the highest manifestation and flowering. Love brings to the fruit of the tree and of the tree of life and of the Word of God the highest meaning of all teachings that have come forth through the I AM Activity, through Theosophy, even through the Bridge to Freedom.

Yes, the highest truths have yet to bear their fruit by the full manifestation of love, which shall be in this activity—love that does impart them and convey such profound understanding that immediately upon hearing the teaching by one empowered with love all souls of light may attain heights of consciousness to which they have not yet reached.

You who would go forth to teach, call for the heart of Jesus and Kuthumi. Call for the heart of Maitreya and the fire. Desire to convey a cup of living flame fit for the person or persons you speak to. Yes, beloved, let this be a company of love in the rapture of love and the communion of saints in the etheric octave.

When you lose the point of love, go to the altar again, sing a song of love, remind yourself why you walk the earth and why you toil. Why do you do anything if it is not to endow the very earth that you plant with love itself?

O Love! Love all that you see and all that you do not see! Love is your empowerment. Love is the flame of eternal life. Love is the seventh ray mingled with the power of the will of God in so many violet-purple hues.

Love is transmutation. Love brings out the best in all whom you meet. Love restores them to the sanity of the Christ mind. True divine love is welcomed by those who have it, even a morsel, or have a memory of it if they have not cultivated it.

True divine love is the judgment upon those who reject it. And the fallen ones in the earth, beloved, detest divine love and anyone who does carry it. In some quarters it is out of style to smile and be happy and exult in the joy of God in heaven. Cynicism is the way, and atheism and the long face and the sternness of mien.

Yes, beloved, love endows the soul with character and the mind with the will to fulfill the profile of the avatars and the saints.

Love is the reason for being of The Summit Lighthouse.

May you be, one by one, a chalice of that love. And as that love descends and touches the untransmuted human sense of love, the human sympathy and empathy, let it consume it. Let compassion reign. Let kindness reign. But let that sympathy and empathy identifying with the lower nature of others be far from you!

You have heard this instruction but I, Saint Germain, repeat it, for I am bringing an endowment of love to this activity this day. And I say it must not be perverted—misused or misqualified or misunderstood.

Divine love raises all to the divine ideal and the divine plan. Divine love is uncompromising. Know this, beloved. It is uncompromising! Thus, many do not understand divine love. Many will accuse you of selfishness when it is divine love in all its power that you are manifesting.

Divine love is coming to the altar of God and directing that fire into the earth. Divine love of the Holy Spirit, as you know from Pentecost itself,[6] is the judgment of abortion and the abortionist, those who abort the divine plan and life in any sector of the cosmos.

Divine love is a two-edged sword that binds the darkness and sets free the lightbearers who have been captives of fallen ones.

Divine love is a mystery that you must find out but you will never do so by taking apart the petals of the flower. Only by allowing the flower of divine love to unfold in your heart will you discover its mystery, and you cannot know the mystery until you do.

Therefore you must trust the mystery of divine love. You must trust it, beloved, to come upon you. You must follow its lead, sometimes blindly, sometimes enduring the pain of returning karma, sometimes wrestling with ages-old momentums of the appetites and passions of the lower self. They will not go away without wrestling!

And you wrestle because you know that the other side of this particular stage prop is the divine Reality of the rose of love.

You pursue it in the darkest night of the soul. In the dark night of the Spirit,[7] you are moving toward the rose of divine love. And when you find it, it shall be because it has opened in your heart because you have determined that finding, seeking, finding, seeking, finding has been worth all of that, all of that to know this mighty rose of light of the heart—yes, the rose of light of the heart.

This activity is the culmination of all others we have sponsored. It is intended to be the culmination of all dispensations that have gone forth in 25,800 years.[8] It can be all that you make it, all that you will it to be, all that you desire. *You* are the physical matrix. *You* are indeed The Summit Lighthouse.

Thus, remember that Archangel Michael did say upon the founding of this organization that this activity does have the greatest potential and endowment of any he had sponsored since he did bring Home the first root race.[9] That is the cosmic matrix. That is the almost unlimited potential of this activity.

And I say "almost," for in the physical octave there is yet limitation of time and space. Yet time and space are the only limitation. And until you have filled time and space with the teachings of the ascended masters as the waters cover the sea, beloved, you shall yet have room for expansion.

It is like your embodiment, beloved—all things are possible. Anything is possible to you in God's will. And this is how you feel in that limitless sense of the child, even the adolescent, even the youth; this is so the world around. Limitations of the body that crop up by its misuse begin to convey a sense of spiritual limitation and mental limitation but this is the illusion invoked by those who misuse the body temple.

I, Saint Germain, speak to you, then, of all that must be done in this decade and of the potential for turning back prophecy.

May you begin again to give certain and specific decrees for the raising up of the physical as well as the spiritual defense of America. May you give these calls to Archangel Michael in a new and shortened preamble, thereby taking upon yourselves once again the labors of Hercules[10] given to you by El Morya, that you might clear the way for the people of this nation to deliver a mandate to their president and their Congress for the immediate deployment of defense against all intrusions upon this nation from those who are gaining weapons of war, nuclear weapons—even the Soviets, who increase those weapons day by day.

Yes, beloved, if you do not give forth the call to Archangel Michael as an absolute God-command out of the flame of peace, holiness, and love in your heart for that defense, you will never know what might have been. And if you make the call and those who are called of God—who can implement its answer as representatives of the military and the government—do not move forward with that defense, you will have upon your record that you have made the call and done the work and therefore will have no karma and no part with those who have decided against defense.

I bid you in this process to consider what the messenger has taught you—that unless you give the call to Helios for the binding of the dweller-on-the-threshold of those individuals who stand against defense, and unless you make the call for the binding of the dweller-on-the-threshold of all citizens of the United States of America, there will not be change. For they, beloved, will remain set in their mental mindsets, set in their fear and doubt whereby they desire to be deceived—set in their allegiance to the powers of darkness, set in their momentums of suicide whereby they welcome a nuclear holocaust, for their time is up in any case.

Yes, beloved, I empower you this day to call for the binding of the dweller-on-the-threshold of those who are Americans—and when I use the term *Americans,* I speak of the lightbearers of the world. I speak of all, whether they are in or out of embodiment, who have the I AM THAT I AM, all who have a threefold flame.[11] Make the call in their name and for them. Make the call for the binding of the fallen ones who prevent their union with God and one another, prevent their enlightenment, prevent their contact with this activity.

You must enter into the Law of the One.[12] Our messenger has taught you this law. And you ought to be grateful for the divine understanding that God is one and Christ is one and, therefore, to call for the binding of the dweller-on-the-threshold of millions or billions of individuals of light or darkness is no greater an effort than to call for the binding of the one.

This is true unto those who understand the Law of the One of their I AM Presence, who understand that they are one in and of the mystical body of God. To know this intellectually is not enough, beloved: you must know the divine Reality of the mathematics of being. You have the power of the One. And when you doubt it, simply meditate upon Jesus Christ, your Lord.

Meditate upon him and think how he has borne the karma of the planet, lo, two thousand years—lo, how he, the singular individual, has brought salvation to the people of this earth, even to those who know it not; how he, the one, the avatar of the age and the ages, has manifested the Light to compensate the Darkness so that you could live and walk the earth, so that the Great White Brotherhood might continue to serve, so that all of hierarchy could intercede in the founding of this Summit Lighthouse!

Yes, think of the One and the one with God who is the majority. Enter that God daily! Consume your misuses of the blue-flame cross[13] and know the power of God that is available to you! And if you must, listen again and again to these dictations and read them and do not forget them, for they are an endowment. They are the founding of and the foundation for the new level of the next thirty-three-year spiral.

Oh yes, beloved, you can do these things. And I promise you that there shall be a judgment upon those who prevent the Lord of the World and the ruby ray masters and ourselves from implementing the divine plan for victory in Armageddon in the physical octave! This is that to which we set our minds and hearts and bodies this day, our wills and our desire.

We know the ultimate victory in Armageddon on inner planes of being. But you have descended to this octave in this life, we have descended to this octave in our former embodiments, and as long as we can occupy these low levels of vibration through you,* we are determined to bring the victory to this level! [32-second standing ovation]

Moreover, we are determined to bring this victory to lower levels and to the astral plane and ultimately to the depths of death and hell itself until these are swallowed up in the conflagration of divine love, because if we do not, some souls will be lost, as Mother Mary has said.[14] Therefore, we *will* bring it into the octaves of hell!

Beware, ye fallen ones, for the hosts of the LORD do march in your canyons this day and the lightbearers march with them!

[23-second standing ovation]

Through the Divine Mother Mary, the Church Universal and Triumphant is the crowning glory upon the Church Militant.[15] Yet the Church Militant has not been militant and the Roman Church has not waged war against the fallen ones but has been taken over by them until the highest ranks of that church are filled and defiled with fallen angels! Therefore, our Church Universal and Triumphant shall fulfill the office of the Church Militant simultaneously with that of the Church Triumphant.

And we are on the march with Sanat Kumara and his legions of light. *We are!* [16-second standing ovation]

The pillar of fire of divine love does descend upon this altar. It is the endowment, beloved. The pillar of fire of divine love shall go before you. The pillar of fire of divine love shall be within you and upon you.

That pillar of fire is for the victory. It is for the confounding of those who move against you. And yet as they do, the waves of love move out and out and out and beat upon the shores of their beings. Either they be converted, beloved, or they shall be consumed in the great consummation of love, which is indeed a conflagration of material cosmos—and there is a fire that does one day restore all things to their spiritual origin.

One day in that point of your origin, sealed with your twin flame in the heart of the Elohim of Love, Heros and Amora, may you know the sense of the satisfaction of having drunk the cup of victory and drunk to the dregs the cup of your karma. I wish you, as my wish upon this

*The masters are in the earth through the bodies of their chelas.

birthday, beloved, the satisfaction of having drunk both and known, in the ultimate sense, that you have walked this earth in the honor of God unto the dishonor and the final judgment of the fallen ones.

I, Saint Germain, prophesy this fulfillment for this activity and that it shall be done through *you* and all whom you shall magnetize to this, our magnet of Love! [24-second standing ovation]

August 11, 1991
Royal Teton Ranch,
Park County, Montana

Saint Germain and his divine complement, Portia, are the hierarchs of the Aquarian age. Together they deliver to the people of God the dispensation for the seventh age and the seventh ray. The seventh ray is the violet ray of freedom, justice, mercy, alchemy, and sacred ritual. As Chohan, or Lord, of the Seventh Ray, Saint Germain initiates our souls in the science and ritual of transmutation through the violet flame. He is the seventh angel prophesied in Revelation 10:7 who comes to sponsor the finishing of the mystery of God "as he hath declared to his servants the prophets." He is also the sponsor of the United States of America, affectionately referred to as "Uncle Sam." Saint Germain, whose name means "Holy Brother," was embodied as the prophet Samuel, Saint Joseph, Merlin, Roger Bacon, Christopher Columbus, and Francis Bacon. Following his ascension in 1684, he reappeared in the eighteenth and nineteenth centuries as le Comte de Saint Germain, the "Wonderman of Europe." Saint Germain's retreat in North America is the Cave of Symbols at Table Mountain, Wyoming. He also teaches at the Royal Teton Retreat, congruent with the Grand Teton, near Jackson Hole, Wyoming.

(See *The Masters and Their Retreats,* pp. 312–22, 430–32; *Lords of the Seven Rays,* pp. 221–55, 493–519; and Virginia M. Fellows, *The Shakespeare Code,* the life-story of Francis Bacon, true author of the works of Shakespeare.)

CHAPTER 15

The Maha Chohan

OUR LAST AND BEST HOPE

Your Mystical Union with God

Because this activity was, and is, our last and best hope for this age, we, the seven, have given to it our all. Our all and highest good is divine love. Therefore that love has descended.

Inasmuch as we knew that there would not be another dispensation forthcoming in the twentieth century from Helios and Vesta or the Four and Twenty Elders for such an activity of the Great White Brotherhood, we determined, beloved, to commit to The Summit Lighthouse so much of ourselves and our causal bodies, along with many unnamed saints of the early Church and those of other dispensations of ages beyond recorded history.

All have contributed. All have determined that we should give a cornucopia of light and love and wisdom and the finest sponsorship and tutoring of hearts and souls that the world could know and has ever known in such dark ages.

Yes, beloved, this is the truth that I speak. This activity is the last and best opportunity for those in embodiment on earth to reach their I AM Presence. You must understand that this is due to the limitation of grants available from the Great Central Sun and to the abuse and misuse of many previous dispensations or the nonresponsiveness of the people to the teachings, now available in so many languages across the bookstalls of the earth and in the homes of many.

Thus, as you understand this in terms of your life and service and ascension, you will see that this activity is also *your* last and best hope and opportunity to fulfill your reason for being, balance that karma and know the supreme soul-satisfaction of bringing one precious heart to the fountain of truth and of his own I AM Presence.

As I did release, as God in me did release, the Paraclete on that day in Philadelphia, so the cloven tongues present on the original Pentecost[1] come nigh to you, beloved. They are at all heights above you. Upon first glimpse they look like seagulls descending, but they are more than seagulls: they are cloven tongues of fire, which represent the great God of the four quadrants and of higher being.

Today the Paraclete does come to give you an added portion according to that which you have given, according to your effort and desiring. The Paraclete does come to help you, as you have strayed from the central thought of love. The Paraclete does come to reinforce the thoughts of love that you have embodied.

O holy love, O holy love, even as the dove of the Spirit, now greet thine own! Let there be the quickening! Let them know, O divine manifestation of God—let them know that without the Spirit there is no life or truth or love, there is no light.

I preach to you as your Lord, the Maha Chohan. I preach to you, beloved. Know the Spirit of the LORD. Be willing to invoke that Spirit and to say:

Prayer for the Invocation of the Holy Spirit

O my Lord, I know not what I shall receive when I shall invoke thee! Nevertheless, I am willing. Even as Elijah did smite the waters and Elisha after him,[2] so, Spirit of God, divide the way of the human consciousness! Smite those waters of the astral body! Purify them! Quicken me!

Yes, I can endure the pain that is required for my soul's rising. I do not fear it. I enter the bliss of God. And I do not deny the necessity of pain as an accelerated alchemy!

But I shall not endure the false pain put upon me by fallen ones. I defeat that by the sword of Maitreya. For I AM the peace-commanding buddhic presence and I wield the sword of the Spirit. I AM in the heart of my Mother, Kali. I AM in the heart and the midst of the circle and sword of blue flame of beloved Astrea. And I AM WHO I AM.

O Spirit of the LORD, Spirit of the I AM THAT I AM of the entire Spirit of the Great White Brotherhood, I come a supplicant. Receive me, O God, this day! Let thy Spirit deliver me from my illusions and glamour, from my vanity of self. Let the Holy Spirit deliver me.

O God, I AM ready this day, as ready as I will ever be, and this moment in time and space I must consecrate to my deliverer and my deliverance. For I know the cups and moments, as thimbles infinite in the finite realm, shall continue to come. And they shall pass by and pass me by and I shall reach the term of years and then no longer have the cup of choice in time and space. I choose, O God, not to postpone it:

This day I AM begotten of thee!

I AM born again!

I mark this day as my new birth.

O Spirit of the I AM THAT I AM, I receive thee now. Receive me, O God. And if I am unacceptable in thy sight, purge me, O God! I am willing to be purged. For there is nothing in this life that means more to me than the bonding of my soul to my God and my Saviour.

I have drunk every cup, known every way, seen the end from the beginning through the mistakes of others and their tragedies. I have seen it all in a thousand and ten thousand lifetimes. I choose this moment to be demagnetized from the gravity and the gravitation of this planetary consciousness.

I shall walk in the Spirit from this day forward and I shall walk in the flesh and blood of my being and I shall know my God. By his grace let my face shine with the inner light, that all may see and know that the light of God in the earth can truly be captured and held in the chalice of a finite being and in the flame that is infinite and unfed in the heart.

I want the world to know that God inhabits his people; therefore I will show it forth in my temple. And though they curse and despise me, they will *know* they have seen my God in my flesh. For I repeat the prayer, "Yet in my flesh shall I see God!"[3]

And if I see that God, I shall project it upon the mirror of this matter manifestation of the whole world! And those who deny it may meet their God and those who affirm it may meet their God. For all shall meet him one day, all shall meet her one day.

Yes, O Spirit of the I AM THAT I AM, I shall never be ready but I AM always ready. I know this mortal cannot be perfected. Therefore, let it be broken and let my immortality be known. I know that I am intended to embody my God. And by the power of the Maha Chohan and his love and wisdom, I affirm my God-freedom from my lower self this day!

Fire of God, consume me unto the consummation of worlds! For I AM the practical mendicant. I AM going forth and I will have my cups filled, ready to give to those whom I meet. I will do it, my Lord.

Beloved, as you kneel once again, you shall receive the fire that is meet for you in answer to your prayer. [Congregation kneels.]

Fear not, for God knoweth thy portion and the portion thou canst contain this day. Fear not. Fear not, beloved, but fear the alternative of the nonreceptive heart. This is that which ought to be feared.

ELOHIM

Therefore, pray ye and overcome thy fear:

Unto thee, O God, do I commend my spirit. Commend thy Spirit unto me and let there be the fusion of worlds in my being this day.

In the beginning of the cycle I did extend the new cup. In this conclusion of the cycle I say: Be thou the new cup! Be thou that cup.

As we came seeking a channel to offer himself to God, herself to God, and we did receive these messengers who would speak what we would say without hesitation, without resistance, so this day we come to seek in you channels for the fount of light whereby those who come to you may receive the cup of cold water in Christ's name of the true teachings of the Divine Mother and the enlightenment of the Holy Spirit.

Cloven tongues of fire quicken your crown chakras as ye are able to receive them. Feel the tingling now and know a new burst of illumination's flame opening the way for your mystical union with God and your enlightenment.

Truly study the Law, study the teaching and, beloved, by the fire of the Holy Spirit, guard the peace! Guard the peace of one another. Should you be the source of the stone of stumbling whereby another does lose his peace because of your spoken word or vibration, then you shall share the guilt with the one who has received that energy and been moved by the very riptide that came through you.

Thus, I seal the message of the Elohim of Peace. Guard the peace in all whom you meet. Nurture the flame of peace. Do it by the Spirit of the Lord. Guard the peace. *Keep* the peace. Keep the peace. Keep the peace.

I am with you alway, unto the fulfillment of Cosmic Christ peace within you. It is the chalice for the flame of divine love.

August 11, 1991
Royal Teton Ranch,
Park County, Montana

The Maha Chohan, or Great Lord, is the representative of the Holy Spirit to earth and her evolutions. Among the qualifications for this office in hierarchy is the attainment of adeptship on each of the seven rays, which merge into the pure white light of the Holy Spirit. The one who bears the office of Maha Chohan presides over the seven chohans of the rays. With the seven chohans, he initiates our souls in preparation to receive the nine gifts of the Holy Spirit, spoken of in I Corinthians 12:4–11. The ascended master who currently holds this office was embodied as the poet Homer. In his final incarnation, he was a shepherd in India who quietly kept the flame for untold millions. The Maha Chohan maintains an etheric retreat with a physical focus on the island of Sri Lanka (Ceylon), where the flame of the Holy Spirit and the flame of Comfort are anchored.

(See *Lords of the Seven Rays,* pp. 523–36; *The Masters and Their Retreats,* pp. 200–3, 471–72.)

CHAPTER 16

El Morya

LET THE WORD GO FORTH!

Two-Thirds of the Original Purpose of the Thirty-Three-Year Dispensation Has Been Accomplished— One-Third Remains to Be Fulfilled through the Delivery of the Word

Take Nothing for Granted

Evermore I AM your Morya El! [38-second standing ovation]

Truly it is a day of righteousness. It is a day of returning to the law of God. And it is altogether fitting that you have come to Summit University this summer to be tutored of the World Teachers and so fitting that you have come willing to be chalices for the ministry of God in this age.[1]

I am gratified, gratified indeed! And my gratitude is now a transmission of fire of the joy of the will of God to your heart. I transmit to you joy, beloved, a joy incomparable: it is the joy of those who live to fulfill that will. Therefore be seated in this joyous flame.

Carrying the blue rose of Sirius on behalf of all who can receive it, I also reminisce with you this day upon those early beginnings. With a certain measure of heaviness on my heart and yet with a great lightness I did explain, on August 7, 1958, how difficult it was to secure the dispensation of The Summit Lighthouse from Helios and Vesta against the backdrop of the failures of many and the burdens that we the brothers in white had borne (and, for that matter, continue to bear) for faithless ones who could not carry the cup of light.

So I did explain at that board of directors meeting in Philadelphia that I did commit on that occasion jewels and other momentums of attainment that I did not care to speak of. Great was the gift of my heart as collateral for that which was to be.

And, beloved, there were so few in the beginning, yet the promise was given for three and another three and a seventh.[2] Thus, there did come from the heart of Archangel Michael the promise as well as the protection of the seven below by the seven who spoke Above.

Now, beloved, we see the fruit of accomplishment. And you may recall that at various points in this movement's history I have again come forth to pledge a certain diamond and a certain momentum[3] that this activity might continue, even when in the dark hours of the storms of the astral sea, the Lighthouse was all but overcome by the waves and the momentums of the dark ones.

The rejoicing I have this day is upon the great victory of many who have surely provided a compensation for my service and a response, who have gotten me benched and unbenched[4] and therefore allowed me to continue.

I can tell you surely, beloved, that when you see burdens continue or calamities in your life or things not moving at as great a speed as you would desire, you can know that I am reaching the limits, almost as though the sky were a canopy and I could not press beyond it. You can know that I have run out of the fire of your decree momentums to my heart and you are bearing a weight that is not necessary, one that I should desire to carry for you but cannot.

It does not matter what day of the week it is, though the Tuesday is preferred, beloved, but for you to consecrate a service to me means that not only can I assist you but others of the ascended host whom I may call upon can also assist you. For I give the energy and the momentum of your decrees to others in hierarchy who also seek the dispensation to assist you. We are bound by the limits of the necessity for you to experience certain of your momentums of karma, certain of your momentums of neglect, but beyond that, beloved, we would bear for you much more than we are able, given your present levels of application to my decrees.*

I therefore return to the point of the discussion regarding individual Christhood. And so we come to the thirty-three-year mark in our history. It was expected and, in fact, required by Helios and Vesta that at the turning of the year thirty-three there should be found in this community souls of light embodying a certain portion of their Christhood—a portion that cannot be defined by me but may not necessarily be required to be the ultimate portion of the full incarnation of the Christ. I speak, then, of disciples well on their way to embodying that Christhood, having the cast of mind of Christ and of what Christ would do in each situation.

Beloved ones, I have sponsored souls in the past year who could fulfill this requirement, some of whom have come to this activity of the Great White Brotherhood with a goodly portion of their Christmanifestation. This has indeed helped the record of the service of all who have been a part of this community.

On the other side of the ledger, beloved, it is necessary, according to the grant of Helios and Vesta, that you make the call for the binding of the dweller-on-the-threshold of all who can swiftly realize their Christhood or a portion thereof and of all of those who have turned against their own Christ Self and therefore against the messenger of that Christ. Thus, to clear the records of those who have come and gone and in their hatred of the Christ cursed the activity itself as well as the messenger—this is an obligation that must be fulfilled, for it is a part of the requirement of the original dispensation.

As that dispensation came forth from Helios and Vesta and as the thirty-third anniversary did approach, so Helios did speak to you, did remain thirty-three days with Vesta in the earth.[5] They came also to secure the original dispensation that it could be renewed in this hour.

Take nothing for granted, beloved. The renewal in this hour had to be pondered, had to be deliberated, had to be agreed upon, this time not alone by Helios and Vesta but by the Four and Twenty Elders and Alpha and Omega.

*"I AM God's Will," decree 10.03, and "El Morya, Thou Chohan of Power," decree 10.09

Therefore, beloved, this celebration and these dictations are indeed a fact because those below, you yourselves and your fervent hearts, and those Above have worked together to see to it that they could be made possible. Therefore, this is our cause for celebration and congratulations to you and the hierarchy of light this day!

[30-second standing ovation]

You ought to know, beloved, that two-thirds of the purposes that were to be fulfilled in these thirty-three years have been accomplished. One-third remains, beloved, and therefore I trust you will see and understand, as the emphasis has come forth in the dictations and from the heart of the messengers, that it is the outreach and the presentation of the teachings in every form and in the media and by your heart-to-heart and person-to-person delivery of the Word that must give the increase, that must bring about the swelling of the ranks, that must spread abroad the true Christ consciousness that many may walk in.

Therefore, it is timely indeed for you to have made your commitment to be here at this time to take the ministerial training course. So many of you applied; and you who have been accepted have prepared yourselves and you have taken a stand with others who have come to Summit University this summer and with those of the staff and the children and the entire world of Keepers of the Flame. You have held steady your oar and kept to your rowing and continuous action. You have secured a foundation. It is a foundation that you have been preparing that this new thirty-three-tiered spiral might come forth.

You have done it, beloved. Now you must carry out that which must be brought into the physical. The conclusion of every cycle is the physical manifestation.

Therefore you have seen all hell break loose to oppose you through many interest groups and spiritual wickedness in high places[6] to prevent the physical manifestation of the purposes of this ranch and of your properties in Glastonbury.

Yes, beloved, the physical battle is being waged. It is being waged psychically and at inner levels and by many individuals unknown to you. You must have the physical victory and you *shall* have it if you continue in your dynamic decrees and understand that this is a moment when you can fulfill that cycle, and its reason for being, of the first thirty-three by the momentum that you have gained in your months and years of service. And this momentum can overlap the beginning of the new. It is a physical challenge that does coincide with the Dark Cycle coming to the physical octave.[7]

All are being tested and have been tested throughout this year and the years past. Yet some have not returned to drink of our fount but have determined to go away in bitterness and in the gall of that bitterness.[8]

Let them be confronted! Let them be turned back! Let them choose to enter the glory and the joy of the new dispensation and to have the good karma of fulfilling the old in the physical plane, else let them go their way!

It is time for the lukewarm to not be present, beloved, for you must be hot or cold![9] And if you wax hot, you will have the power of the yin and the yang. And if you wax cold, you will have the power of the yin and the yang. But if you wax lukewarm, you shall have neither, for the polarity of being and the divine dance of Lord Shiva is based upon the T'ai Chi and only this.

Therefore, my beloved, let there be the pruning again of the rose bush[10] and let you go forth,* my beloved, to the four corners of the earth to be a beacon light of our Summit Lighthouse.

Yes, I have come. And I stand with the stalwart ones and I stand with the weak and the undecided. For at this moment of our anniversary I stand by all, the frail and those who God-identify.

I have come to help you and to give a final opportunity to those of you who are halfhearted. I, Morya, cannot carry you much longer. Therefore, repolarize yourselves to the magnet of divine love in my heart and know the renewal of your being. It is an hour of renewal by the Holy Spirit, by the Elohim of Peace, by the violet flame of Saint Germain, by the protection unending of Archangel Michael, who has delivered you personally and carried you in his arm so many times.

---

*As noted in *Webster's Third New International Dictionary,* the use of *let* to form the second-person imperative is common in Ireland.

O beloved, is this, our Summit Lighthouse, not the love tryst of the ages where heaven and earth meet and you know the glow of a perpetual springtime of love even while the enemy rages?

[Audience replies, "Yes!"]

Yes, beloved, sing to the springtime of love! Remember your youth and the Eternal Youth, Sanat Kumara, and his holy ones. Remember the fullness of the sacred fire in your temple. Remember to keep the LORD's covenant and to keep it holy.

I have stood with Saint Germain at the Royal Teton Retreat and in counsel with the Lords of Karma, yes, beloved, and Mother Mary with us. We are deeply concerned as to the conditions in the world and have profound regret that though the messengers have spoken, though we have spoken, the threat of Soviet Communism and the intent of the leadership of the Soviet Union has not been perceived by the people or their leaders.

I reiterate the call for you to give the decree for the binding of the dweller-on-the-threshold of those of the I AM Race, those who are Americans at heart wherever they are on the face of the earth.[11] Let them be cleared! Let the fallen ones be bound! And let this message *pierce* and *penetrate!*

Let the people dream the dreams of God and see reality in their sleep. Call that they might be shown in the Cave of Symbols and the Royal Teton Retreat what is the true equation. Call for the lightning of the mind of God to pierce their density! Let them be compelled by the seven archangels to see that reality in a glimpse and then again and again and again until Reality does haunt them and finally they embrace her as their deliverer.

God-reality is profaned by those who abuse that sign of Libra in their treachery and in their intrigue and in their deception.[12]

Oh yes, beloved, the mission of The Summit Lighthouse was, and still is, to quicken the people of all nations and to inform them as to the intent of the International Capitalist/Communist Conspiracy. And as the messenger has said, its message has made her and this activity unpopular.

Yet we must care for our own. We must reach out.

Do you regret that you have borne the embarrassment of your messenger's message, beloved? ["No!"]

I thank you for this, for some would have surely preferred not to have their leader so maligned and ridiculed.

Yes, beloved, it has borne fruit, for the lightbearers have come apart. They shall be saved. And this was the design of our dispensation.

Yet, beloved, in unleashing the dispensation of The Summit Lighthouse we desired more, even the quickening of the entire earth, and so did Helios and Vesta. And Helios came to the July 1991 conference with the express purpose of seeing why there has not been greater general acceptance of the teachings of the ascended masters through these messengers and this activity.

His conclusion, which he has given to the Darjeeling and Indian Councils and at the Royal Teton Retreat, is that not enough preparatory work has been done by our shepherds and chelas in plowing the field of consciousness, in invoking the violet flame and making the calls again and again for the binding and setting aside of the carnal mind and the dweller-on-the-threshold of the children of the light and the sons and daughters of God. Your calls preparing the way for souls of light to come into this activity could have made the difference in the response of some individuals, turning their negative to a positive.

Now you have that call[13] and a mighty momentum on it, and it does work more wonders than you dream of. Thus, Helios himself has determined to further endow that call and those who give it with his power of the sun and the power of his original dispensation of this community.

For The Summit Lighthouse is more than an organization. It is the community, the Sangha, of the Buddha. It is the Dharma of the Buddha. And it is the Buddha itself. These Three Jewels,[14] these three, take refuge in them, in the very person of the Buddha, the Buddha whom you see.

Whom do you see, beloved?

Do you see Gautama? Do you see Sanat Kumara, Maitreya? Do you see your Christ Self? Do you see the budding Buddha within you?

Take refuge in the Buddha you can see, even as the messenger has taken refuge in my heart and in the lineage of hierarchy she represents.[15] Yes, beloved, meditate upon the God whom you can see and you shall become that one.

Yes, this is The Summit Lighthouse. It is awareness by the three dots.* Now you know: the three dots are the Sangha, the Dharma and the Buddha. I take my refuge in them, which means I take my refuge in your heart, beloved. Your heart is the place of the inner Buddha, even as your I AM Presence is the Buddha.

I take refuge in the heart of my chela. Where else can I go in this world? I tell you nowhere—nowhere but to the heart of the chela who does intone, "Not my will, not my will, not my will but thine be done!" —words of Christ,[16] words mocked in the media, as though this will could be the human will of the messenger. It *is* the will of the messenger in that it is the will of God that the messenger does adore and seek to become.

It is only the will of God that guides this activity. And if you are concerned lest the will of God be not manifest in some corner of its operation, I say, call to me!

Am I not concerned, as you are?

Of course I am. You must be my eyes and ears. You must make the call. You must demand the exposure. You must be willing to tell the messenger! The messenger's bodies are fully occupied with matters pertaining to this octave; therefore sometimes things are not seen or noticed unless called to her attention.

It is well. It is well. It is well.

Many of those who were a part of the beginnings, those gray heads who came to me from other activities in those bygone days, have made the transition, have gone to etheric octaves, some taking their ascension, some returning. And I celebrate their rebirth in this community with great rejoicing! I am a grandfather and a great-great-great-great-grandfather many times over to the same souls, beloved! And I enjoy it to the fullness of my office.

Now then, let the Word go forth, as it always has, without compromise. Let the Word go forth from the archives of the lectures of the

*Often El Morya signs his name with a script letter *M* with three dots.

messengers! Let souls qualify themselves as *good* editors, *good* writers, *good* compilers of information, whose work is sufficient and well done.

Yes, beloved, you who have drunk from the fount must pass to others that stream unending. Let the Word go forth, for this is part of the unfinished business. We cannot bury the Word in the napkin[17] of our filing cabinets and think that we do God service. Yes, all words that have been spoken are intended to be assimilated and heard and read as the Everlasting Gospel and to be the dividing of the way in society in the midst of those conditions which, when exposed and brought to the attention of many, will draw a certain action from below and Above.

Through all of this, beloved, I thank you. I am grateful this day that we are here together in one place in the harmony of God in the presence of the Holy Spirit, that we *do have* a new dispensation to go forward. I tell you, beloved, for this my God-gratitude is unending. And I only say to you, let the fount rise! Let the Christhood descend! And may you fulfill the fullest measure of the original dispensation that you might prosper and be rejuvenated and regenerated by the next.

I am with you always. May your call come to me, even as you have answered my call from the beginning.

Now, therefore, I, Morya, send forth the call to all the earth, and by the shaft of light of the Summit beacon it reaches the hearts of all who are impelled this day to follow that light.

May you cut them free daily by your swords of blue flame! This is my request as I bow to the light within you and return to Darjeeling Council meetings regarding the serious state of world affairs.

[18-second standing ovation. Audience gives the salutation:]

Hail, El Morya! Hail, El Morya! Hail, El Morya!
Hail, El Morya! Hail, El Morya! Hail, El Morya! . . .

August 11, 1991
Royal Teton Ranch,
Park County, Montana

The ascended master El Morya is Chohan of the First Ray (blue ray) of God's Will and Chief of the Darjeeling Council of the Great White Brotherhood. He is the founder of The Summit Lighthouse and the Guru and sponsor of the messengers. The master's extraordinary devotion to God's Word and Work is a powerful stream that has run throughout his incarnations on earth. Among his recent embodiments are the patriarch Abraham, Melchior (one of the three wise men), King Arthur, Thomas Becket, Thomas More, Akbar the Great, the Irish poet Thomas Moore, and the Rajput prince El Morya Khan. El Morya is the hierarch of the Retreat of God's Will in the etheric plane over the city of Darjeeling, India, in the foothills of the Himalayas. Together with members of the Darjeeling Council and the Brothers of the Diamond Heart, he assists sons and daughters of God in implementing the will of God as the blueprint of every project. Statesmen, executives, lawyers, teachers, and leaders in all fields of endeavor are schooled at his retreat between embodiments and in their finer bodies during sleep.

(See *Morya and You* (three volumes), *The Chela and the Path,* and *The Masters and Their Retreats,* pp. 87–92, 474–77.)

CHAPTER 17

Gautama Buddha

I DELIVER THE UNCONDITIONED LOVE

A Time for a Great Battle: A Time for a Great Victory

Look unto the Source! Look unto the Source!

Return to your point of origin.

The cosmic balance of your activity is the Great Central Sun. Lo, Alpha and Omega! See them Above, see them below.

Are you not the mirror of the Central Sun? Can you not visualize now a giant dish, a reflector, reflecting back to you in manifestation all that I AM in the Great Central Sun of Being?

See how a cosmos as an inverted umbrella may manifest through you. See how that mirror can so contain and reflect the Presence of God as Spirit that that power shall be unto you to defeat those who by their distorted consciousness have mirrored the perversions of fallen ones—of angels who have attained to high levels yet turned against their point of origin. This is an original act of suicide by the fallen ones that is not completed until their expenditure* of all that which they have been and their receipt of all that which is due them according to the Great Law as opportunity to repent, as compensation for those good works that are yet to their credit.

*their outpicturing

Thus, the long duration of Evil, beloved, has been by the manipulation of the Law by the fallen ones, who have made certain to tie humanity to themselves, presenting themselves as benefactors, sponsors and therefore always causing society to be indebted to them. Thus they manipulate the Law, beloved. Yet their time is short,[1] for they do have a karma for this manipulation, and their works are not done to the glory of God.

Now, if you will enlighten the children of God and those among humanity who will listen to you because you take the facts and figures of life as it is today and prove to them what are these sowings of the seed of the Wicked One, you may be able to deliver the children of God and humanity from their awkward dependence upon the fallen ones, to separate them out from them, and to let the fallen ones fall by their own weight.

Yes, the deliverance of the children of God from indoctrination and the false ideologies of the fallen ones—it is a mighty work, it is necessary! Yet I tell you the good joy of your effort. It is this, beloved: One child of light turned around counts for many, for it is the Law of the One. And that one at his level of being and karma has access to all those vibrating at that same plane.

There is a multiplication, beloved, and the fruit of your sowings with the messengers in these years is yet coming to harvest. The harvest shall be great and the fallen ones know it and they seek to ruin the harvest by manipulation of weather and elementals so that you cannot reap the abundance of joy and the souls whose time is long due to be here.

All of the Law is on your side. All that you know about making the call on the signs in the skies of the astrological configurations, all that you need to know to defeat that which seeks to defeat you is in your hand.

I, your brother in the path of the Buddha, recommend that you become as fierce as Kali and "super yang" for a while, and that you fight that fight against the powers of darkness with a fierceness from this King Arthur's Court and in every place to which you shall return this summer's end.

Yes, beloved, it is a time for a great battle! It is a time for a great victory! Our forces are ready: all of my armies in defense of the Buddha in every soul upon earth—my armies who defend the threefold flame and who move to stand guard lest those who have it lose it by a trick of the force and a turn of their hand.

Yes, all are ready—Sanat Kumara and his legions, the Faithful and True, the Lord Jesus Christ. Yes, all have their armies, beloved. There is, in fact, not a saint or a master in heaven who does not have some company of angels that protects his mission and those who serve with him. The more chelas that gather around a single ascended master or saint, the more that one has to plead before the Lords of Karma for servants and armies and seraphim to take care of those who are the faithful.

Oh, the cosmic scheme of things! I am in wonder of it again and again! As I perceive the glory of the heavens and all those stars* whose starlight descends as a gentle rain upon your auras, as I see the capacity for you to break through the consciousness of limitation and mortality, I tell you, there is such an opportunity waiting for you just around the corner—yes, for you who have made those mistakes and who wallow in the sense of guilt!

Oh, give that sense of guilt to me this day! For our Lighthouse of Love is intact and that love is surely unconditioned. It cannot be conditioned but it is not unconditional, beloved. It is unconditioned by the human consciousness. Yet it comes by merit and that love always is the sword of discrimination.

I say to you, put all human consciousness of guilt in the flame of my heart this day; for this day is indeed an open door, as we have told you. This is a wondrous day for new beginnings. Contemplate the mystery of a new thrust of spiral and a new dispensation. Contemplate the magnitude of it and see yourself at its very nucleus and at its nadir.

Understand, then, to ride this spiral is most advantageous. And you who know the law of cycles will not fail to lock yourselves, each one, as one with this spiral, to make yourselves even tight to your body so the body can spin and the body can be a part of the inner chamber of this giant spiral of light, and you can travel through it in another dimension and in another body and contain it.

Your God contains it! Your Christ contains it! You are that God,

*the immortals

that Christ. You are that Buddha. There is nothing more to say when we have said this, beloved. Everything else is surely a development of this theme.

I AM the theme of Buddha this day. I AM that theme, that theme of the sound of the tone of your inner Buddha, the seed of light in your I AM Presence.

I am surely the one to remind you: Think Alpha and Omega! Will you not put up signs to remind yourselves? Let your thought glance above you in moments when you must have the precise answer—lest the enemy unhorse you in this round.

I am in many levels of being, presenting myself in all planes. I occupy simultaneously the etheric octave and the octaves below. I will not allow it to be that souls of light or darkness do not confront me on a daily basis.

They must see me. They must know me. They must see my smile and laughter mocking their ways or praising them on, one or the other. They must see my face in you and in little child. They cannot escape the gaze of the Buddha upon them through you. Lightbearers must see my eyes. Fallen ones must become enangered and enraged and know that it will not avail them a single thing.

Yes, beloved, I am determined that they must look at me. And as I move through the messenger, the messenger is also determined that they must see and know—and deny if they will and affirm if they will. But the dividing of the way of Light and Darkness is the mission of the avatars and yourselves as bodhisattvas.

Who among you has taken the bodhisattva vow? Tell me now!

I assure you it is more among you than have raised your hands, for you have indeed determined to become disciples of the Buddha. And in one sense of the word this is the definition of *bodhisattva.* And I count you as my disciples and I know that you count me as your Buddha. Is it not so? [Audience replies, "Yes."]

Then let us see again who has chosen the bodhisattva path. Why, all of you, of course, beloved, all of you! It is true. It is true! It is true! And therefore, Helios and Vesta have indeed given the renewed dispensation for The Summit Lighthouse this day.

Then take the vows of Kuan Yin.[2] "I desire/I vow to quickly know the entire Dharma!" Yes, the fullness of the Dharma. Yes, the fullness of the Way. It is all right to vow this, beloved. It is safe! It is safe. Take refuge in the Buddha, the Dharma, the Sangha.[3]

Will you take refuge in outer darkness? I ask you. ["No!"]

Well, then, what other choice have you? There is the circle of the One, and outside of it, it is like the darkness of spaces unknown.

Yes, you can take refuge. Yes, you can be imperfect. But remember, you were called upon at this July conference to select a single virtue to outpicture in this life.[4] As this dictation was given, instantly the messenger saw the virtue that is her own and that she must continue to espouse. And that single virtue returned to by her daily is the guard of consciousness and like the rudder of her ship calling her back to the duty of her office.

How many here heard and saw the virtue of their calling, espoused it and have continued to see that name above them?

Not all, beloved. But you may do it this day. Your Holy Christ Self will tell you what is the special virtue on which you have a momentum and what is that same virtue that you must therefore complete. You should not select a virtue in which you have no attainment. This would not be wise. Therefore, realistically assess yourself. Step apart from yourself. Observe yourself in your daily service. What one quality comes to mind that you know you embody when all else fails?

That is the one, beloved. That is the one. It is something that others will count on in you, something that you may already be known for among your fellow bodhisattvas. Yes, beloved, it is there. I assure you that that jewel in your being is your link to my heart and to the Sangha and to the Dharma. If you did not have it, you would not be here.

Then search and find it. Polish it, cut it and polish it again. Every day fulfill a requirement of that virtue and you will soon find yourself with greater attainment on one of the lines of the clock and then all of them. For a virtue of God will enhance your ability to embody all of the attributes of God.

Virtue, then, is to be sought. And I tell you, it would be interesting to note, if you could write it down on a piece of paper, what you perceive as the virtue chosen by God for the messenger, chosen by the messenger unto God—what is the one virtue that you depend on in the messenger and that you appreciate. Then turn to yourself and say: "I want to be depended on to keep one petal of the thousand-petaled lotus of Gautama Buddha. I want people to know that when this virtue is needed I am there, I uphold it, I keep that flame."

Thus, with a thousand of you each holding a petal, some duplicating the same virtue, of course, there would be the making of such a lotus, such a thoughtform over our sangha, such an assurance to many upon earth that you were walking with this in mind and that you kept that single flame, that single flame of the crown chakra. This petaled flame, beloved (and this is the secret of the reward), by its very nature—by the very fact that it is God—attracts all others. And your keeping of this "virtue-flame" is the key to the opening of the thousand-petaled lotus in the sangha and in yourself.

And should you journey to the level of Maitreya and his bodhisattvas,* you should know that each one would shine to you with such a quality of a virtue as to make that virtue unmistakable in its identification.

Yes, beloved, when you have that virtue you can see that with it is your victory. And with the human qualities that yet abide and remain, there is that need for constancy and one-pointedness to keep that single virtue, and it eventually will swallow up all other manifestations that you desire to have swallowed up in the flame—the flame of enlightenment.

I speak of a virtue as a point of enlightenment, for you must have a point of enlightenment in order to desire to embody a virtue and to make it your own. This is how you ascend. This is how you balance karma. Because the rock of your strength and all of your striving is in keeping that single point of flame.

Know the difference between a virtue and a quality of God and an attribute. The attributes of which we speak are on the twelve lines of the clock. The qualities of God are portions of those attributes. But a virtue is a single petal of a quality itself, like faith or hope or charity or honesty or directness or sincerity. There are many, many qualities that you may describe, which yet come down to the single petal of a virtue.

*Lord Maitreya and his bodhisattvas maintain their sangha retreat at the twelfth level of the etheric octave.

A virtue has the capacity to embody the allness of God and of Buddha. And as you recite the vows of Kuan Yin, I promise you, beloved, that those mantras shall become a moving force from the levels of the unconscious and the subconscious, superconscious and conscious minds.

Though you may have trepidation about giving them, though you may feel not ready for those vows, I tell you, you are ready. And that which trembles in fear, beloved, is simply the untransmuted self, those levels of the four lower bodies that know that in your becoming the Divine One you will shuffle off those finite forms and become the full manifestation of the Sambhogakaya and the Dharmakaya.[5]

Therefore, to give up the house of habitation here below does cause a certain trembling. Yet, as a bodhisattva of higher attainment, even after your ascension, you may be allowed to embody in the Nirmanakaya to appear to those who need you. This is the Way and the Path.

Thus, do not underestimate the force of planetary fear or unconscious fear that is not a part of your soul or spirit or mind or heart but a part of the very vibration of the octave in which you live. This octave has a static of fear and anxiety that comes with it. Thus, do not become confused by this fear and consider then that because you have that uncertainty you should delay and postpone giving the mantras of the bodhisattva vows of Kuan Yin.

These mantras are of your true being, your true desiring, your divine Reality, of which your soul was once a part until it did go forth. And it did go forth deeper and deeper into the astral sea. And in some cases the delicate thread of contact was broken and in other cases the threefold flame was snuffed out, and farther and farther away have you and others roamed.

And the way back, beloved, is to take the bodhisattva vow.

This is the meaning of our Summit Lighthouse. This is the meaning of our Church Universal and Triumphant. If you know in divine Reality—and you know that you know it—that in the purity of your God-free being you desire the return, then I say use those mantras and take the vows daily and you shall see how you become the center of a spiral nebula.

And, beloved, the fire infolding itself,[6] as from all of cosmos, shall draw unto you, internalizing and infolding within you every point and increment of light, energy, consciousness, intelligence, supply, abundance, love, purity that you need to become the embodiment of the bodhisattva who is the disciple becoming the Buddha.

You see, beloved, the fallen ones have programmed the compartments of the mind and the four lower bodies with the anti-mantra. Every song they sing out of hell, of rock music, so many sayings, so many teachings piled layer upon layer upon layer—these are their programmings. They are programmings of the anti-mantra, the anti-vow! You see, they deny even that molecule that is the formula for your identity of being.

When God says he does plant a seed in you, he means he is planting the seed that is the molecule of your identity and the key to it. And when he plants that seed in you, he seals it untouchable. Then by neglect, by forgetfulness, by the calcification of the mind, it becomes the lost formula of the lost chord of your being.

Now, that seed, beloved, is planted even in the crown chakra or the base chakra or the heart. The fallen ones attempt to crack that formula and then to pervert it so that you do not know yourself, you cannot find yourself, you cannot find the key to your God-reality. Yet the seed has been planted. It is sealed until it will be safe for you to find it, until you are wise enough not to reveal it to anyone, not to allow it to be seen by the fallen ones—until you are wise enough to know you need that unending protection of Archangel Michael.

A high percentage of this planet is in the astral plane and you move in that sea. Yet you are not of it; you are of the etheric octave. You are from Above and not beneath.[7]

I tell you, beloved, the vows of the bodhisattva Kuan Yin will displace the anti-Word of the fallen ones. They know this secret! Therefore have they stood between you and your taking of the vows of Kuan Yin. This is how they have enslaved you! This is how they have caused you to forget your origin, of which your messenger reminds you again and again. The memory of who you are has been lost, erased, displaced. And you have been left vulnerable by your own departure from the honor of God, the honor of God as his white fire in the higher octaves.

Thus, would you reconnect to the thread of contact that leads to the stream of life of God? ["Yes!"]

Understand, this is how you do it: you must make the vow. But the vow you have already made long ago and then you did forsake it. Truly, I tell you, in your heart of hearts and true being of soul you desire that vow but you do not connect with that desire. It is because of this, beloved: The leopard does not know that he has spots. Individuals are not aware of the density that has overtaken them. They do not see their way out. That is why the Guru comes as the Dispeller of Darkness.[8]

I AM that Guru to you! And I lower that mantle upon this messenger. I have placed the mantle of the Lord of the World upon her. It is a heavy mantle. It does protect and empower at once.

You cannot see what you have lost. I tell you this day what you have lost: the formula of your identity and that formula manifest in your four lower bodies.

The vows of the bodhisattva are peculiar mantras, unique. They will re-create and manifest the molecule of your identity yet seal it in the very fire of the mantra itself that it may not be touched.

Mark me well, beloved, should you begin this day and continue even with one mantra a day of the vows of the bodhisattva, you shall come to this place this day and date next year to look back upon that cycle and you shall know that my words are true and that something has changed in you at the most profound levels of your being. And you will be delivered from the force of the fallen ones who return to the point of vulnerability in your four lower bodies to replay for you again and again your past sins, your past hurts, your past pains and all that has been done to you.

These replays are the anti-mantra, beloved. They will not go away until you displace them. Many mantras we have given you will assist the process, but those do not require a commitment. How can God return to you the formula of God-free being unless you vow to return to him and on the way be the saviour of sentient life?

Is it hard for you to "kick against the pricks"[9] of your Lord and Saviour Jesus Christ? Is it hard, beloved?

I tell you, when you resist the coming Christ you make life very difficult for yourselves. You choose the hard way. Yes, it is very hard to kick against the Christ who comes to save you.

Why not embrace your Lord this day? Never has there been a more opportune moment in these thirty-three years. Embrace your Lord, recite the vow and be free at last from the struggles of your own psyche and psychology—all of that which has been programmed into you by various fallen ones sent as family members, as personages in your life in this and previous lifetimes to make a mess of hell out of your four lower bodies from which you could not untangle yourself, so complex, then, has the labyrinth of the subconscious become.

Yes, beloved, the path of the bodhisattva is the key. I open now the octave of Maitreya and his bodhisattvas, who smile upon you, who send you their joy and their laughter. And they say to you, beloved, "We are here because we have recited our vows. You are there because you have not recited your vows!"

Yes, enjoy and be enjoined by their laughter. Is it not funny? Yes, it is, beloved. This is the rejoicing today, that the heavens are opened and you see them above.

Now see what they are doing, beloved. They, the ones of compassion—bodhisattvas of compassion with their Buddha—they will not be moved in pity or sympathy for you. But what are they doing?

Each one has a rope that is wound on a device. And you see these ropes coming down and they are coming down upon your heads and into your hands as they uncoil them. These ropes come a long way in terms of vibration, beloved. But in terms of distance, it is up to you to create* that distance and to narrow it.

Thus, unmoved in their etheric octave of light, they extend the rope. If you hold on to that rope, one day they shall wind you up and take you higher and higher. You must have the ability to hold on to the rope. Who can hold on to the rope for any length of time without an assist, without something to stand on?

*i.e., to determine

It is difficult, beloved. The key is in the recitation of the vows of the bodhisattvas under Kuan Yin, the open door. The key is to understand that the Guru in embodiment is here to support you as you hang on to the rope and are carried aloft by your own momentum. The bodhisattvas extend the rope but you must make your way and provide the energy for them to crank you up again.

Such a glory of God is the unconditioned love that I deliver once again as the foundation and the fulfillment of your Summit Lighthouse and ours! [29-second standing ovation]

Messenger's comments:

I, the messenger, say to you in the name of Gautama Buddha, seize and claim your rope in this hour! For your name is written on it and your bodhisattva above has vowed to keep the flame and balance for you. If you do not claim it, another may well take it. Therefore, seize the moment and seize the rope!

Seize the rope and pull it to your heart. Fasten it to your heart and rejoice. Rejoice in the path of the Guru-chela relationship. Rejoice in the path of bodhisattvas, who care and care so completely as to understand their office of noncompromise that allows them to help us.

This is the beauty of Lord Gautama Buddha and the beauty and truth of his flame, the flame with which he endowed the foundation of The Summit Lighthouse.

Feel the beauty of his presence and feel beautiful in God forevermore. And be the sculpture of this form and self until it does embody and reflect the full glory of our God Gautama Buddha.

August 11, 1991
Royal Teton Ranch,
Park County, Montana

Gautama Buddha holds the office of Lord of the World (referred to as "God of the Earth" in Revelation 11:4). At inner levels, he sustains the threefold flame of life, the divine spark, for all children of God on earth. *Buddha* means "the Enlightened One" (from the Sanskrit *budh,* "awake," "know," "perceive"). Gautama attained the enlightenment of the Buddha in his final incarnation as Siddhartha Gautama (c. 563–483 B.C.). For forty-five years he preached his doctrine of the Four Noble Truths, the Eightfold Path and the Middle Way, which led to the founding of Buddhism. Gautama Buddha is the sponsor of Summit University and the hierarch of Shamballa, an etheric retreat located over the Gobi Desert. In 1981, Gautama established an extension of this retreat, called the Western Shamballa, in the etheric octave over the Heart of the Inner Retreat at the Royal Teton Ranch.

(See Gautama Buddha, *The Masters and Their Retreats,* pp. 111–15, 467–70.)

CHAPTER 18

Godfre

WE STAND WITH YOU!

We Bring the Full-Gathered Momentum of Our Causal Bodies to This Activity

As I was called by Helios and Vesta to conclude the addresses of the seven on August 7, 1958, I did come with the full momentum of my service to life not only in the I AM Activity and in the founding of this nation but in all previous incarnations. I am a brother very close to you, having lived in this twentieth century, having found Saint Germain, as he did find me and call me.

You can know, then, beloved, that I bring the full-gathered momentum of my causal body to this activity, as does Lotus with me. And on this occasion we are permitted by cosmic law to lower into manifestation, as a working reserve of energy and supply, new levels and layers and momentums from our causal body—and not only ours, beloved, but the causal bodies of those who have ascended through the I AM Activity and through other past endeavors of the Great White Brotherhood.

Because of you, beloved, we are able to do this—and because you stand and still stand with this messenger. Yes, beloved, you have stood and declared your position in defense of the dictations. You, time and again, have been willing to decree by the hour to deal with the opposition to our coming.

Contemplate, then, this day the opposition to these seven dictations, which did rest upon the body of the messenger and which you did lift by your service, by your love, by your inner and outer understanding of this equation.

The greater the light to be delivered, the greater the opposition. And when you deal with it in dynamic decree, then we do not have to offer our precious energies in defense of our messenger and our dictations, but we may use them to get dispensations for *you* in your path of chelaship and initiation.

Understand that the beginning of the path of discipleship is the beginning of the appellation *bodhisattva,* but its culmination is in the fulfillment of a manifest Christhood. And that Christhood is the springboard to the attainment of Buddhahood, which is the full manifestation of your I AM Presence. Thus, from the beginning to the end of our sayings this day you are indeed called to manifest that fullness of your God-free being.

I can tell you that without Saint Germain and the ascended masters I would not have gotten my victory over the beast of human creation. Therefore I say, declare this day that you are *through and done with that human creation* by the full fervor and fire of your being and see how the hosts of the Great White Brotherhood shall come to reinforce your declaration!

I give you some moments now to make the greatest fiat of your life unto the very courts of heaven.

[Congregation delivers powerful fiats unto God for liberation from the tyranny of the human consciousness and its human creation.]

So I am reminded of the day and date when I turned on my human creation. And, yes, beloved, had I not done so, I should have had to reincarnate and not known the fullness of the victory of my ascension. None can do it for you and only when you have done it do you know the full intimate relationship that you can enjoy with the ascended masters.

Yes, beloved, you are the doer in this tango. Yes, indeed, beloved! It is a divine romance and a divine dance with the Lord Shiva and with a cosmos itself. Yes!

I will not say to you, "What are you waiting for?" For you are not waiting except in the sense that you are brides-in-waiting for the full consummation of your love.

I therefore make known to you that all that has been drawn forth by the decrees of the I AM movement is consecrated to the victory of this Summit Lighthouse, this Church Universal and Triumphant. It is another reservoir of light to be added to the one to which you contribute daily by your decrees. [19-second standing ovation]

I AM God-free in the thousand-petaled lotus of my heart and crown, and my beloved Lotus is eternally free in the God-freedom that I emblaze upon her and upon all of you. And we are one and we have transcended our human propensities.

Know us, then, in the fullness of the light and know that we stand with you! For as it has been said, *you* are our best and our last hope for the redeeming of all that we have contributed to this mighty stream of divine love descending to the chalice of hearts of light on earth.

Everyone who has ever walked the earth and contributed to the victory of an age or a community, every one will echo my sentiments from the octaves of light: You are the last and best hope for the fulfillment of our respective missions,* which remain unfulfilled until the full victory of love is won.

Therefore I say to you in the words of the Goddess of Liberty and quoted by your beloved El Morya, "March on!" March on, beloved! Do not fail to continue the march, for you have all the support of heaven to fulfill the nine points of the Law and the next thirty-three steps. They will be the telling of the future of earth.

We are confident in the victory. May you retain that confidence.

All of heaven blesses and seals you in this hour. And I, Godfre, am never absent from this property or heart, nor is Lotus with me.

With an endearing and enduring love, we seal this day and this momentum. Now it is yours to run with.

Oh, run with it, warriors of the Spirit! Be not confined except to do the will of God, his love, his wisdom, his purity, his honor.

[33-second standing ovation]

---

*the mission of the I AM Activity and the mission of The Summit Lighthouse

Messenger's Invocation:

We are grateful, O God, for this day as the day of the dawning of a new reality, the dawning of a new opportunity. Let our heaven be on earth and our earth be in heaven. Let us not be separated for a moment from thy octaves of light or from our brothers and sisters caught in the web of darkness.

We are The Summit Lighthouse, O God, and we shall walk the earth as that Lighthouse as long as thou art with us and we with thee in the keeping of our vows.

Seal us, O God. Seal this light. Seal all that is released in the great sphere of light over this property, in our causal bodies, that all that has been given this day and all that is behind it back to the Great Central Sun might be meted out to us day by day unto the fulfillment of this thirty-three-year spiral.

Let many receive an extension of life to be here all of the days of the thirty-three years to come, O God. Strengthen us as we strengthen ourselves.

Hercules and Amazonia, be with us—El Morya and Lanello. Let angels of God and fellow brother and sister remind us and by love's own promise help to keep us in the narrow way, where we are always beneath the sun of our I AM Presence and not in the shadows of that human creation, which we have disavowed this day.

We have disallowed it, O God! We stand firm by our fiat! Send us angels to help us and bind whatever of our human creation we cannot see each day. And let the substance of density pass away, O Lord.

I am grateful thou hast called me in this life, O God. I am grateful for the sacrifices made on behalf of my victory and service by ascended masters and angels and most especially by my fellow chelas on the Path, my brothers and sisters, my family. O God, I am grateful for the support of all those who have given their love and dynamic decrees in my behalf. I ask to serve them in a greater capacity even as they serve thee with all the love of their hearts.

In the name Jesus Christ, I command the hosts of the LORD to bring to resolution all attempts by the federal, state, or local government or any other group, pressure groups, the press, the media, et cetera, to tear from us our mission, the right use of our property and our resources, including our geothermal well, and let divine love resolve and dissolve all matters in dispute.

Let my people go, O God, that we might continue to sacrifice unto thee, to serve thee, to surrender unto thee, and to be selfless in the presence of thy Great God Self, which is our divine Reality!

O beloved Lanello and beloved El Morya and the masters and angels who assist you, I thank you for raising me up and pulling me out of the mire of my karma and human creation. I thank you for raising up all who are here.

We ask for your continuing support, O God, that we might fulfill the promises and redeem the hopes of all who have gone before us who will know their crown of victory when the two-thirds mark of our founding dispensation reaches the hundred percent and beyond.

O God, let us all balance that karma that we might bring home much, much light and more of a causal body to offer at the feet of the Lord of the World and all who have sustained us. For thy saving amazing grace, O God, we are so grateful. And now we are so grateful to receive thy Holy Communion.

Therefore we call to you, Lord Jesus, to bless the bread and the wine. As it has absorbed the light of these dictations, so as we take it we assimilate the Lord's Body. For it is the physical sign, symbol, and chalice of the living Christ come again into our bodies in this moment.

In the name of the Father, the Son, the Holy Spirit, and the Divine Mother, I seal this light in the Christ Self of each one and in the chakras of those who are able to retain it in harmony and to good productivity as laborers in the field of the Lord. Amen.

[Holy Communion is served.]

Benediction:

In the name of the Father and of the Son and of the Holy Spirit, in the name of the Divine Mother, I AM the sealing of these hearts in the mighty protection of Archangel Michael, the peace of Elohim Peace, the violet flame and cup of love of Saint Germain, the empowerment of the Holy Spirit, the Paraclete, the fervor of the will of God of our beloved El Morya, the peace-commanding presence of Gautama Buddha, the rescue of the lightbearers through the vow of Kuan Yin and by the rope of the bodhisattvas of Maitreya, and the mighty momentum of Godfre and Lotus and the students of the I AM THAT I AM and our beloved Lanello.

By the power of the Cosmic Christ, it is done, it is finished, it is sealed. Amen.

August 11, 1991
Royal Teton Ranch,
Park County, Montana

The ascended master Godfre and his divine complement, Lotus, were embodied as Guy and Edna Ballard (1878–1939 and 1886–1971 respectively). In the 1930s Saint Germain contacted the Ballards and trained them as his messengers. Through them, the master founded the I AM Activity and released the dispensation of the violet flame. Under the pen name Godfré Ray King, Guy Ballard wrote *Unveiled Mysteries* and *The Magic Presence,* in which he tells of his experiences with Saint Germain and gives basic teachings in cosmic law. Godfre made his ascension on December 31, 1939, having won his immortal freedom through his obedience to the laws of God. Lotus ascended on February 12, 1971. Among Godfre's other embodiments were Richard the Lionhearted, king of England (1157–1199), and George Washington, first president of the United States (1732–1799). As an ascended master, Godfre ensouls the consciousness of God-obedience, charted on the 4 o'clock line of the cosmic clock under the solar hierarchy of Taurus. He is a master of buddhic attainment.

(See *The Masters and Their Retreats,* pp. 116–17.)

NOTES

CHAPTER 1: • Obedience to Love

Preceding the dictation, the messenger delivered her lecture "Karma, Reincarnation and Christianity." (See 1992 *Pearls of Wisdom,* vol. 35, nos. 11–14, 17, 22.)

1. John 14:18.
2. John 14:23.
3. Refiner's fire. Zech. 13:8, 9; Mal. 3:1–3; Matt. 3:11, 12; Luke 3:16, 17.
4. Exod. 20:3; Deut. 5:7.
5. John 13:34; 15:12.

CHAPTER 2: • Self-Discipline on the Path to the Ascension

1. Mal. 3:1–3.
2. John 13:23, 25; 21:20.
3. Seek adeptship. See Archangel Michael, "New Beginnings," 1991 *Pearls of Wisdom,* vol. 34, no. 47, pp. 541–42.
4. The four personalities of God. See *Saint Germain On Alchemy,* pp. 72–73, 271–77 (1993 pocketbook), pp. 62–63, 233–38 (2019 trade); *Predict Your Future,* pp. 38–40; and *The Human Aura,* chap. 6, pp. 141–52 (2015 pocketbook), chap. 6, pp. 149–63 (2015 trade).

CHAPTER 3: • The Mirror of Truth

1. Mother Mary, Queen of the Angels, is the archeia of the fifth ray and the divine complement of Archangel Raphael.
2. Ps. 90:10.
3. The retreat of Elohim Hercules and Amazonia is on the etheric plane in and over Half Dome, a huge, mile-high rocky dome in Yosemite National Park, California.
4. John 9:5.

CHAPTER 4: • So Great a Love

1. Heb. 2:3.
2. *siddhis* [Sanskrit, roughly translated as "perfect abilities"] and *vibhutis* [Sanskrit, literally "revelations, powers"]: supernatural powers acquired through

---

Bible references are to the King James Version. Books referenced in these notes are published by Summit University Press unless indicated otherwise; available at Store.SummitLighthouse.org.

the practice of yoga. These include clairaudience, clairvoyance, the ability to read thoughts, knowledge of previous births, levitation, dominion over the elements, and the ability to make oneself invisible.

3. Luke 17:20, 21.
4. In 1206 Saint Francis was called by God to repair the Church, which had fallen into corruption. While he was in prayer in the ruined chapel of San Damiano outside the gate of Assisi, he heard a voice from the crucifix above the altar command: "Go, Francis, and repair my house, which, as you see, is falling in ruins." For two or three years, Francis dedicated himself to repairing the chapel of San Damiano and two other small churches. In 1209, with a band of eleven disciples, he officially began his Franciscan Order of Friars Minor (the "little brothers") "to follow the teachings of our Lord Jesus Christ and to walk in his footsteps."
5. I Cor. 15:31.
6. The deathless solar body is the wedding garment (referred to in Matt. 22:1–14) that the soul must wear if she is to enter in to (1) the alchemical marriage (the soul's permanent bonding to the Holy Christ Self) and (2) the ritual of the ascension (the Christed one's permanent fusing to the I AM Presence). See "The Great Deathless Solar Body" in *Dossier on the Ascension,* pp. 154–59.
7. Universities of the Spirit. See *The Masters and Their Retreats,* pp. 410–11.

CHAPTER 5: • "Forgive and Be Forgiven"

1. The mantras of Kuan Yin are recorded on *Kuan Yin's Crystal Rosary: Devotions to the Divine Mother East and West,* 4-audio CD album of hymns, prayers and ancient Chinese mantras that invoke the merciful presence of Kuan Yin, the Bodhisattva of Compassion, and Mary the Mother of Jesus. Includes "Ten Vows of Kuan Yin," taken from the Great Compassion Heart Dharani Sutra; "Kuan Yin Mantras for the Woman and Her Seed," using sacred names, titles, and mantras of Kuan Yin arranged according to the fourteen stations of the Aquarian cross; mantras to the "Thirty-Three Manifestations of Avalokiteśvara as Kuan Yin." Available at Store.SummitLighthouse.org. *Kuan Yin's Crystal Rosary* booklet is available separately. See also "Special Purpose Kuan Yin Mantras," no. 673 in *Church Universal and Triumphant Book of Hymns and Songs.* For teachings by the messenger on Kuan Yin and her mantras, see:

   "The Ten Vows of Kuan Yin for Our Discipleship under Maitreya," in 1984 *Pearls of Wisdom,* vol. 27, Book I, Introduction, pp. *37–43.*

   "The Path of the Divine Mother East and West: Mother Mary and Kuan Yin," Part I, February 14, 1988: Teachings and mantras on the Immaculate Heart of Mary and the Merciful Heart of Kuan Yin; thorough introduction to Kuan Yin as the Compassionate Saviouress. Available at AscendedMasterLibrary.org.

   "The Path of the Divine Mother East and West: Mother Mary and Kuan Yin,"

Part II, April 17, 1988: Teachings on the Person and Principle of the Divine Mother as Teacher, Initiator, Comforter—from Mother Mary, Isis and Kuan Yin to Tara, the Shekinah and the Hindu Feminine Deities. Available at AscendedMasterLibrary.org.

Thirty-Three Manifestations of Avalokiteśvara as Kuan Yin: Contains teachings and meditations on the mantras of the thirty-three manifestations of Avalokiteśvara/Kuan Yin; how to use the mantras for spiritual healing. A 3-DVD set plus bonus audio CD, includes lecture "The Cross of Divine Love and the Not-Self"; available at Store.Summit Lighthouse.org.

2. Souls with Jesus in ancient days. See Elizabeth Clare Prophet, "The Golden Age of Jesus Christ on Atlantis," available at AscendedMasterLibrary.org.
3. Matt. 22:21; Mark 12:17; Luke 20:25.
4. Join in the mission of mercy for elemental life! Get your own copy of the 2-audio CD set *Violet Flame for Elemental Life—Fire, Air, Water and Earth;* available at Store.SummitLighthouse.org.

CHAPTER 6: • I Plant the Seed of the Ruby Ray in the Chalice Prepared

Preceding the dictation of the Buddha of the Ruby Ray, the messenger led the audience in "Heart Meditations for Those Who Would Be Candidates for the Ascension."

1. Sanat Kumara, Hierarch of the planet Venus, is known as the Ancient of Days (Dan. 7:9, 13, 22). Millions of years ago, in earth's darkest hour, when all light had gone out in her evolutions and cosmic councils had decreed the dissolution of the planet, Sanat Kumara volunteered to come to earth to keep the threefold flame of life on behalf of her people. One hundred and forty-four thousand souls from Venus volunteered to come with him to earth to support his mission. They vowed to keep the flame with him until the children of God would respond and turn once again to serve their mighty I AM Presence. Four hundred who formed the avant-garde were sent ahead to build the magnificent retreat of Shamballa on an island in the Gobi Sea (now the Gobi Desert). There, Sanat Kumara anchored the focus of the threefold flame, establishing the initial thread of contact with all on earth by extending rays of light from his heart to their own. This retreat, once physical, was withdrawn to the etheric octave in subsequent dark ages. (See *The Masters and Their Retreats,* pp. 322–29, 467–70.)
2. Acts 7:48; 17:24; II Cor. 5:1.
3. Archangel Michael called you to seek adeptship. See this volume, chapter 12, p. 108. "Yes, beloved, seek adeptship! It has been said. I say it again: Seek adeptship. Above all, do not make the single mistake of being satisfied with yourself as you are today. And I shall tell you a secret of the seven archangels: We are not satisfied as we manifest God today, and on the morrow you shall see seven archangels in a new manifestation!"
4. Matt. 28:18.

5. Chelas enlisted in Archangel Michael's legions. See 1985 *Pearls of Wisdom,* vol. 28, no. 10; and *The Masters and Their Retreats,* pp. 230–33, 472–74.
6. Phil. 4:3; Rev. 3:5; 13:8; 17:8; 20:11–15; 21:27; 22:19.
7. John 9:4, 5; 12:35.

CHAPTER 7: • Lessons Learned

The messenger's lecture, "Profile of Ernon, Rai of Suern," delivered prior to the dictation is published in the 1991 *Pearls of Wisdom,* vol. 34, no. 60, and is available at AscendedMasterLibrary.org.

1. The lost sheep of the house of Israel. When Jesus left his golden-age civilization on Atlantis 34,500 years ago, two million souls followed him. They went to Suern, present-day India. One million of these souls ascended from Suern. The other million continued to reincarnate, some among the Suernis and some on Atlantis in the realm of the Poseid. Thirteen thousand years ago, the Suernis rebelled against their ruler, Rai Ernon. Those of the one million who were incarnated in Suern did not rebel. However, they, too, were subject to the doom the Rai pronounced upon the Suernis: to dwindle and wait for ninety centuries and suffer until the time of Moses. He told the Suernis that at that time they would be called "the seed of Abraham," the twelve tribes of Israel. The one million who had been with Jesus on Atlantis reincarnated in the tribe of Joseph through his sons, Ephraim and Manasseh, whom Jacob blessed as his own. The tribe of Joseph was one of the ten tribes of the Northern Kingdom of Israel. Today, these one million are reincarnated principally among the peoples of the British Isles, the United States, and Canada. The Suernis reincarnated in the remaining nine of the ten tribes of the Northern Kingdom of Israel and in the two tribes of the Southern Kingdom of Judah. Today, those nine tribes of the Northern Kingdom are generally reincarnated among the European nations as Christians, whereas the two tribes of the Southern Kingdom (Judah and Benjamin) and some Levites are generally reincarnated among the modern-day Jews. For reasons of karma, the seed of Abraham have also reincarnated in every nation.
2. Matt. 15:24.
3. Rev. 3:4, 5; 4:4; 6:9–11; 7:9, 13, 14; 15:6; 19:14.
4. Jer. 31:33; Heb. 8:10; 10:16.
5. Misuses of the sacred fire. The ascended master El Morya teaches his chelas that oral sex is a perversion of the sacred fire and that those who so misuse it are squandering the light necessary to weave the deathless solar body. Hence, they cannot make their ascension following an embodiment of such practice. However, if they cease the practice when they receive this teaching, they may be able to conserve the life force and still attain union with God in the ritual of the ascension at the conclusion of this embodiment.
6. The powerful calls you give. Jesus Christ dictated the decree "I Cast Out the Dweller-on-the-Threshold!" for the express purpose of providing the faithful with the means to overcome the not-self of their own creating. The

dwelller-on-the-threshold must be bound before the Christ can descend into the body temple. This is the meaning of the Second Coming. See decree 20.09 in *Prayers, Meditations and Dynamic Decrees for Personal and World Transformation.*

CHAPTER 8: • The Power of Change

1. Rags for riches. God wants your misqualified energy. In order to receive the scepter of power, you must be willing to give to God your misuses of power in ten times the amount of the value of the gift.
2. Josh. 24:15.
3. Mount Kailasa. The 22,028-foot "Jewel of the Snows" in the Himalayan range, southwestern Tibet; revered by Hindus as the paradise of Shiva and his consort, Parvati.
4. The Maxin Light is the unfed fire that burned in the temple of Incal on Atlantis for five thousand years. The flame, which cast "a light of intense power," burned in the shape of a giant spearhead, over three times the height of a tall man, as described by Phylos the Thibetan in the book *A Dweller on Two Planets.*
5. The descent of the Holy Spirit's judgment. See the Maha Chohan, February 22, 1988, "The Mandate of the Holy Spirit: Love's Testing of a Planet and a People," in 1988 *Pearls of Wisdom,* vol. 31, no. 29.

CHAPTER 9: • Light Cycles of the Decade

Prior to the dictation, the messenger delivered her lecture "Prophecy and the Current Crisis." See 1991 *Pearls of Wisdom,* vol. 34, no. 63. For a biographical note on Saint Germain, see this volume, chapter 14, p. 132.

1. In this dictation Saint Germain draws a distinction between Light (capitalized) and light (lowercased). The Light/light of the Great Central Sun is both the light-emanation of the physical sun center of the cosmos and the Light-emanation of the God/Christ/Buddhic consciousness. It is light in the physical sense of energy/electricity/lightning and Light in the sense of the God Presence, Christ Presence, and the Buddhic Presence. For the most part, in the Matter universe, Light always contains light but light does not always contain Light.
2. The planting of the seed in the chalice prepared. See the Buddha of the Ruby Ray, "I Plant the Seed of the Ruby Ray in the Chalice Prepared," this volume, chapter 6.
3. Rev. 11:18.
4. *manvantara* [Sanskrit]: one of the fourteen intervals in Hinduism that constitute a *kalpa,* a period of time covering a cosmic cycle from the origination to the destruction of a world system. In Hindu cosmology, the universe is continually evolving through periodic cycles of creation and dissolution. Creation is said to occur during the outbreath of the God of Creation, Brahma; dissolution occurs during his inbreath. See 1988 *Pearls of Wisdom,* vol. 31, no. 45, note 7 and encyclopedia.SummitLighthouse.org/manvantara.

5. Isaiah's prophecy of the coming of the child. In Isa. 7:14, Isaiah proclaims to Ahaz, king of Judah: "The Lord himself shall give you a sign. Behold, a virgin shall conceive and bear a son and shall call his name Immanuel." Some commentators hold that this prophecy referred to a child to be born in the near future—possibly Hezekiah, the firstborn son of Ahaz; or Maher-shalal-hash-baz, the second son of Isaiah. The traditional Christian interpretation is that the prophecy referred to the coming of Jesus Christ. Some scholars believe that it referred to both a contemporary child and the future Messiah. The ascended masters' teaching on Isaiah's prophecy is that it is specific to Jesus Christ but it also denotes the divine archetype of the Manchild of Revelation 12. The universal Christ comes forth from the womb of the Cosmic Virgin, and his presence is born in the hearts and souls and spirits of the people when they are ready to receive him. The sign of the Divine Manchild appearing within each one is the sign of the individual's endowment with the consciousness of the Cosmic Christ. It is also true that avatars are born in every age—or a single avatar for each two-thousand-year period. Therefore, the prophecy is pertinent to us in that our Saviour, Jesus Christ, was born to be the avatar (incarnation of God) for the age of Pisces. Because he was born and lived and has carried our karma these two thousand years, we are saved. The sign of the Divine Manchild appearing is also the call to each and every one to give birth to that Christ consciousness through the individual Holy Christ Self under the sponsorship of Jesus Christ. Thus, the signs and wonders of his appearing may be made known through us as we are his disciples and follow in his footsteps to the full realization of the Word, which he did incarnate.
6. "Beloved Cyclopea, Beholder of Perfection," decree 50.05, in *Prayers, Meditations and Dynamic Decrees for Personal and World Transformation.*
7. The dispensations of the violet flame announced by Omri-Tas and me. See Saint Germain, "The Outline of a Maltese Cross," 1991 *Pearls of Wisdom,* vol. 34, no. 26.
8. The Wonderman of Europe. See *Saint Germain On Alchemy,* pp. xi–xxxi.
9. The great heartache of Ernon, Rai of Suern. See "Lessons Learned," this volume, chapter 7; and the lecture by Elizabeth Clare Prophet, "Profile of Ernon, Rai of Suern," 1991 *Pearls of Wisdom,* vol. 34, no. 60.
10. Leaven hid in three measures of meal. In Matt. 13:33, Jesus spoke the following parable: "The kingdom of heaven is like unto leaven, which a woman took and hid in three measures of meal, till the whole was leavened." There has been much scholarly controversy concerning this verse. Some interpret the leaven as representing the Gospel's penetration into the world, while others see it as indicating apostasy in the Church. In his commentary on this verse, the Reverend C. I. Scofield says: "Leaven, as a symbolic or typical substance, is always mentioned in the Old Testament in an evil sense.... Leaven is the principle of corruption working subtly... and is defined by our Lord as evil doctrine [as in the 'leaven of the Pharisees and of the Sadducees,'

Matt. 16:6, 11, 12; Mark 8:15]." He interprets the parable of the leaven as constituting a warning that "the true doctrine, given for the nourishment of the children of the kingdom, would be mingled with corrupt and corrupting false doctrine, and that officially, by the apostate church itself." We disagree with Scofield's teaching on this matter. Leaven (from the Latin *levare* "to raise") is a substance, as yeast, used to lighten dough. Leaven, or yeast, will leaven both good bread and bad—both the nourishing bread and the poisonous bread. As *The Interpreter's Bible* points out: "Although Paul and the rabbinical writers always use leaven as a symbol of evil influence and teaching, Jesus does not hesitate to employ it to describe the kingdom. . . . The three measures are three seahs, a very large amount. This perhaps calls attention to the vastness of the world, which the kingdom must transform, secretly and irresistibly. . . . The kingdom of Christ is silent and imperceptible, like yeast. . . . But the kingdom, though silent, is yet dynamic. It is a yeasty ferment. It is a quiet revolution. No area of earth is left untouched by the redemptive trouble of its coming. . . . In your heart and mine, and in the customs and institutions of our time, the leaven is at work. We should not fear the gentle agitation or the persistent change. The spirit of Christ is yeast in our world." (See *The Scofield Reference Bible,* p. 1016 nn. 3, 4; and *The Interpreter's Bible* [Nashville: Abingdon Press, 1951], 7:417.) The ascended masters teach that the leaven is the fullness of the Christ teaching and consciousness. The universal Christ consciousness must enter three planes of being—the etheric (memory) body, the mental body and the desire body. When sealed in these three planes of being (the three measures of meal), the Christ consciousness and teaching leaven the whole loaf of our physical consciousness, the planet, and the universe.

CHAPTER 10: • O the Violet Flame!

1. The opportunity of Helios and Vesta. See 1991 *Pearls of Wisdom,* vol. 34, nos. 11, 40.
2. The Sacred Ritual for Transport and Holy Work, Ashram Ritual 5, is intended to be given just before retiring. The ritual assists the soul in performing world service while out of the body during the hours of rest. See *Ashram Notes,* pp. 41–59; *Ashram Rituals* booklet, pp. 33–34, 39–52.
3. In her prophecies the messenger has explained that the decade of the 1990s comes under the influence of the conjunction of Saturn, Uranus and Neptune in Capricorn, which occurred in February 1988. This rare conjunction last occurred in 1307 and inaugurated a century marked by war, famine, economic hardship and the black plague, which wiped out one-third of the population of Europe. The messenger has pointed out that astrology and history repeat themselves. We can expect to see any or all of these same conditions in the nineties because of the similar astrological configuration. See Elizabeth Clare Prophet, *The Astrology of the Four Horsemen,* pp. 110–15 and *Saint Germain's Prophecy for the New Millennium,* pp. 149–73.

4. The ascended masters teach the following way to bless water or any liquid: Hold your glass in the left hand and place the right hand over the top of the glass, palm down. The left hand is the Omega, the receiver, which extracts impurities from the liquid. The right hand is the Alpha, the giver, with which you charge it with light as you give a simple prayer. Ask in the name of your mighty I AM Presence and Holy Christ Self for the liquid to be demagnetized of all toxins, pollutions, impurities and then charged with the light of God. Call to the angels to bless it with the specific healing properties you need for the healing of every cell and atom of your being of any negative condition, known or unknown. Call forth and visualize the violet flame charging that liquid and changing it into a violet-flame elixir of light.
5. Violet flame as a physical flame. See Saint Germain, 1984 *Pearls of Wisdom,* vol. 27, no. 61: "The violet flame is a physical flame! And what do I mean when I say this? I say the violet flame is closest in vibratory action of all of the rays to this earth substance, to these chemical elements and compounds, to all that you see in matter. And therefore, the violet flame can combine with any molecule or molecular structure, any particle of matter known or unknown, any wave of light, electrons, or electricity. Thus, the violet flame is the supreme antidote for food poisoning, chemical waste, toxins, pollution of drugs in the body. . . . The violet flame is the supreme antidote for physical problems. Wherever chelas gather to give the violet flame, there you notice immediately an improvement in *physical* conditions!"
6. Matt. 5:23, 24.
7. Give the bija mantras and Sanskrit intonations. See "Bija Mantras to the Feminine Deities" (available at AscendedMasterLibrary.org); the *Heart, Head, and Hand Decrees* CD, which includes bija mantras, and *Chakra Meditations and the Science of the Spoken Word* (available on MP3 format), both available at Store.SummitLighthouse.org. See also *Church Universal and Triumphant Book of Hymns and Songs,* nos. 617 and 618.

CHAPTER 11: • The Call of Love

1. Matt. 22:1–14.
2. See Saint Germain, the Maltese-cross formation, 1991 *Pearls of Wisdom,* vol. 34, no. 26, pp. 348–49; and Omri-Tas, the violet-flame sea of light, this volume, chapter 10.
3. See Igino Giordani, *Saint Catherine of Siena—Doctor of the Church,* trans. Thomas J. Tobin (Boston: Daughters of St. Paul, St. Paul Editions, 1975), pp. 35, 36.
4. "Chaos and Old Night" is a phrase found in John Milton's epic poem *Paradise Lost* and is often used by the ascended masters to refer to periods in earth's history where destruction, anarchy, war, deterioration, despair, and cataclysm were prevalent on earth. The Goddess of Liberty explains: "Thus with the going out of the light of the nucleus of the God Star itself, there have come periods of darkness and misapplication of the Law, followed by

chaos and Old Night and deterioration. The desolations, as the cold winds crossing the desert, have in their own time and space made the human consciousness itself a wasteland devoid of the cosmic connection with the God Star." (1980 *Pearls of Wisdom,* vol. 23, no. 34) The Elohim Peace tells us that "Our God has not intended the grayness of the planet to turn to darkness and blackness and despair whereby even the finest of souls are devoured by the creeping and crawling things that come out of the depths of the astral plane. . . . Include in your decrees . . . that the darkness of chaos and Old Night shall cease! and that the ravages of the demons and fallen angels in the earth shall cease!" (1995 *Pearls of Wisdom,* vol. 38, no. 16) Gautama Buddha states: "Thus, beloved, we do not decree downfall, chaos, darkness and Old Night. We decree a victory of great magnitude for those who are of the bands of light. We await, then, the choice and the decision and the response of all lightbearers in the earth." (1987 *Pearls of Wisdom,* vol. 30, no. 24)

5. See Og Mandino, *The Greatest Salesman in the World* (New York: Bantam Books, 1968).

CHAPTER 12: • New Beginnings

1. Gen. 5:22–24; Heb. 11:5.
2. Jesus' final embodiment. After his Palestinian mission, Jesus walked the earth in the resurrection flame, passing from the screen of life in Kashmir, India, in 77 A.D. at the age of 81. Following this, his final embodiment, he ascended from Shamballa. (See Elizabeth Clare Prophet, *Maitreya on Initiation,* p. 62; and Gautama Buddha, 1990 *Pearls of Wisdom,* vol. 33, no. 2, p. 22.)
3. Thomas à Kempis, *The Imitation of Christ,* trans. Leo Sherley-Price (London: Penguin Group, 1952).
4. I Kings 19:12.
5. Capricorn relates to the knees. The twelve signs of the zodiac relate to various organs and parts of the body. On the cosmic clock, the hierarchy of Capricorn is charted on the 12 o'clock line of God-power. The abuse of God's power manifests as criticism, condemnation, and judgment.
6. *Archangel Michael's Rosary for Armageddon,* a service of prayers, decrees, and hymns to invoke the assistance of Archangel Michael, the hosts of the LORD, and the nine choirs of angels for the resolution of personal and planetary problems, and for the binding of the forces of evil attacking the children and youth of the world; available on audio CD at intermediate or slow pace. *Archangel Michael's Rosary* booklet is available as a separate purchase. Also *Devotions, Decrees and Spirited Songs to Archangel Michael,* on audio CD at devotional pace; and *Blue Lightning is Thy Love: Dynamic Decrees to Archangel Michael,* on audio CD, all available at Store.SummitLighthouse.org.

CHAPTER 13: • I Inaugurate a Thirty-Three-Tiered Spiral of Peace

1. *virya* [Sanskrit]: variously translated as "vigor," "energy," "strength," "manliness," "zeal," "power," "diligence." In Buddhist teachings, *virya* is one of the

ten *paramitas* ("perfect virtues") that one must practice and perfect as a prerequisite to the attainment of bodhisattvahood. See Elizabeth Clare Prophet, 1984 *Pearls of Wisdom,* Book II, Introduction, pp. *3, 5–8; Maitreya on Initiation,* pp. 41–47; *The Buddhic Essence: Ten Stages to Becoming a Buddha,* pp. 88–90.

2. Chalice of the resurrection flame in the Heart of the Inner Retreat. On June 27, 1987, during Freedom 1987 in the Heart of the Inner Retreat, Archangel Chamuel and Charity announced that a tangible chalice was being formed, tended by Paul the Venetian, Nada, and angels of love. They said: "When the chalice shall rise to meet and greet the Elohimic level, then shall Elohim pour into this chalice that which ye seek, beloved. . . . It is the purging, purging of all impurity: light, then, solidifying and codifying the Word within you." Beloved Alpha explained on July 5, 1987, that the building of the chalice "must give to us entrée to earth twenty-four hours a day by the Spirit of Elohim." On July 13, Elohim Apollo and Lumina said: "As this chalice does rise and has risen that two-thirds of the way to our octave, we await the completion by the breakthrough of resurrection's flame." Calling for an intense decree vigil to the resurrection flame by Keepers of the Flame for the completion of the chalice, the messenger explained that this chalice, "as a 'funnel' of crystal light," would be "the perpetual open door for Elohim to work through all true lightbearers of the world." On August 17, 1987, the Divine Mother Kali announced "the fulfillment of the chalice in the Heart of the Inner Retreat to the Elohimic level." See 1987 *Pearls of Wisdom,* vol. 30, no. 31, p. 302; no. 32, p. 310; no. 37, p. 374; no. 38, p. 383; no. 44, pp. 417, 418; no. 47, p. 443; no. 50, pp. 456, 459; no. 51, p. 461.
3. On the cosmic clock, the blue-flame cross is formed by the 12/6 and 3/9 axes. The qualities of God-power, God-harmony, God-reality and God-control are charted on the clock on the 12 o'clock, 6 o'clock, 9 o'clock and 3 o'clock lines under the solar hierarchies of Capricorn, Cancer, Libra and Aries.

   12 o'clock, Capricorn, God-power, perversions: criticism, condemnation and judgment, all black magic.

   6 o'clock, Cancer, God-harmony, perversions: indecision, self-pity, self-justification, emotional instability, all misuses of the sacred fire and perversions of the Mother flame.

   9 o'clock, Libra, God-reality, perversions: dishonesty, intrigue, treachery.

   3 o'clock, Aries, God-control, perversions: conceit, deceit, arrogance and ego, intellectual and spiritual pride.

   For diagrams and further teaching on the cosmic clock, see Elizabeth Clare Prophet, *Predict Your Future: Understand the Cycles of the Cosmic Clock,* pp. 29–54.
4. The sign of the cross. See decree 10.10, "Blue Cross–Blue Flame Protection," in *Prayers, Meditations and Dynamic Decrees for Personal and World Transformation.* See *Blue Lightning is Thy Love: Dynamic Decrees to Archangel Michael,* on audio CD, or *El Morya, Lord of the First Ray: Dynamic Decrees with Prayers*

and Ballads for Chelas of the Will of God, on MP3 audio CD, booklet included. All available at Store.SummitLighthouse.org. When giving the "Blue Cross–Blue Flame Protection" decree, you make the sign of the cross before you, behind, to the left, to the right, beneath, above, and over the heart center, visualizing blue-flame crosses sealing your physical and spiritual protection.

CHAPTER 14: • Our Magnet of Love

1. John 15:20.
2. Eph. 6:16.
3. Cup of liquid Light. In *Unveiled Mysteries,* Godfré Ray King relates the story of how Saint Germain appeared to him while he was hiking on Mount Shasta and offered to fill his cup with a "refreshing drink" that came "directly from the Universal Supply, pure and vivifying as Life itself." In other instances, Saint Germain offered him a crystal cup filled with this liquid Light. On one occasion, a crystal cup of liquid Light formed in Godfré's hand, which he then offered to David Lloyd, whom he also met on Mount Shasta. Saint Germain has given this drink of liquid Light to others, though we do not have the record. (*Unveiled Mysteries,* 3rd ed. [Chicago: Saint Germain Press, 1939], pp. 3–4, 14–15, 73, 236–42)
4. The Royal Teton Retreat, congruent with the Grand Teton near Jackson Hole, Wyoming, is the principal retreat of the Great White Brotherhood on the North American continent. This physical/etheric retreat is an ancient focus of great light where the seven rays of the Elohim and archangels are enshrined. The Lords of Karma, Gautama Buddha, and all members of the Great White Brotherhood frequent this gathering place of the ascended masters and their disciples while also maintaining the specialized functions of their own retreats. The Lords of Karma meet at the Royal Teton Retreat biannually, at the turn of the year and at summer solstice, to review petitions from unascended mankind and to grant dispensations for their assistance. Conclaves attended by thousands of lifestreams from every continent, who journey there in their finer bodies through soul travel while they sleep, are also held at this retreat as well as smaller classes and tutorials. Here also Saint Germain and Lord Lanto with the ascended master Confucius (Hierarch of the Royal Teton Retreat) are conducting their universities of the Spirit—courses of instruction being given by the lords of the seven rays and the Maha Chohan at their respective retreats for tens of thousands of students who are pursuing the path of self-mastery on the seven rays. See *The Masters and Their Retreats,* pp. 462–65, for a detailed description of the Royal Teton Retreat and its activities.
5. Lanello on clearing the etheric quadrant. See Lanello, 1989 *Pearls of Wisdom,* vol. 32, no. 8.
6. The fire of Pentecost for the judgment of abortion. See Jesus, 1991 *Pearls of Wisdom,* vol. 34, no. 18. Note: In June of 2022, the U.S. Supreme Court reversed its 1973 decision (Roe v. Wade) legalizing abortion.
7. In the ascent to perfection, the soul passes through what Saint John of the

Cross describes as the "dark night." The first dark night is experienced as one encounters the return of his own personal karma—the human creation that almost completely obliterates for a time the light of the Christ Self and the I AM Presence. This "dark night of the soul" is in preparation for the dark night of the Spirit, which involves the supreme test of Christhood faced by Jesus on the cross when he cried out, "My God, my God, why hast thou forsaken me?" In this initiation, the soul is completely cut off from the I AM Presence and the heavenly hierarchy and must pass through the crucifixion and the resurrection, sustained solely by the light garnered in his own sacred heart, while holding the balance for planetary karma. For the messengers' teachings on the dark night, including readings and commentary on the writings of Saint John of the Cross, see Elizabeth Clare Prophet, *Living Flame of Love,* 2 MP3 audio CDs; *The Path of the Universal Christ,* pp. 189–93; both available at store.SummitLighthouse.org; and "The Dark Night of the Soul," a lecture delivered on April 12, 1974, available at AscendedMasterLibrary.org.

8. 25,800 years. Elizabeth Clare Prophet, *Saint Germain's Prophecy for the Millennium,* pp. 149–73. The 25,800 years of mankind's karma delivered by the Four Horsemen concluded on April 23, 2002.
9. A root race is a group of souls, or a lifewave, who embody together and have a unique archetypal pattern, divine plan and mission to fulfill on earth. According to esoteric tradition, there are seven primary root races. The first three root races have won their immortal freedom and ascended from earth. The fourth, fifth, and sixth root races (the latter not entirely descended into physical incarnation) remain in embodiment on earth. The seventh root race is destined to incarnate on the continent of South America in the Aquarian age. Each root race embodies under the aegis of a Manu, who is the Lawgiver and who embodies the Christic image for the race. Lord Himalaya and his divine complement are the Manus for the fourth root race; Vaivasvata Manu and his consort are the Manus for the fifth root race; the God and Goddess Meru are the Manus for the sixth root race; and the Great Divine Director and his divine complement are the Manus for the seventh root race. See *The Path to Attainment,* pp. 278–95, for a detailed history of the root races.
10. Labors of Hercules. During the 1989 harvest conference, *The Twelve Labors of Hercules,* Archangel Michael announced that Hercules and the seven Elohim had come to give decree assignments, known as spiritual labors, to the attendees. During the conference, the messenger and chelas worked on these 12 spiritual labors corresponding to the 12 labors of Hercules in Greek mythology. The decree assignments were for the binding of astral forces and fallen ones attacking the lightbearers and for penance, initiation, and the balancing of karma. The *Twelve Labors of Hercules* conference is on 4 DVDs and 1 MP3 audio CD, and includes all the dictations and a lecture by the messenger on the meaning of the 12 labors of Hercules; available at Store .SummitLighthouse.org.
11. The word America is composed of seven letters, which form the words I AM

Race, signifying a "race of lightbearers" descended from Above—from the I AM Presence. These lightbearers of all nations retain the inner memory of the individualization of the Godhead identified to Moses as I AM THAT I AM (Exod. 3:13–15). They carry the seed of the I AM THAT I AM within their hearts.

12. Law of the One. In *The Lost Teachings of Jesus,* Book One, chapter two, "The Point of Origin," Mark Prophet explains the Law of the One. "You are children of the One and God is that One. In his oneness he created all of us as a part of himself. Simply stated, we are all cells in the universal body of God and in him we live and move and have our being. In him we have our Identity. Outside of him we have none. And that God Identity is one, the same One for you and for me. But we're all very different expressions of that One and by our individual expressions we define his oneness, even as he defines our own." (paperback, pp. 58–59; trade, p. 48)
13. Misuses of the blue-flame cross. On the cosmic clock, the blue-flame cross is formed by the 12/6 and 3/9 axes. Both the qualities and perversions of God-power, God-harmony, God-reality, and God-control are charted on the clock on the 12, 6, 9, and 3 o'clock lines under the solar hierarchies of Capricorn, Cancer, Libra, and Aries.
14. Souls will be lost. In a dictation given April 9, 1989, Archangel Raphael and Mother Mary gave the following report: "There are souls being lost daily who are caught in the astral consciousness, 'fixed' . . . to the television set, which does feed into them astral effluvia and does take from them light. . . . Souls who began with a threefold flame are losing their threefold flames. They are reaching the point of the squandering of the light where that divine spark is either about to go out or has gone out already." (1989 *Pearls of Wisdom,* vol. 32, no. 34)
15. In Catholic theology, the Church Triumphant is the Church in heaven; the Church Militant is the Church on earth, which is engaged in constant warfare against the powers of Evil.

CHAPTER 15: • Our Last and Best Hope

1. Acts 2:1–4.
2. II Kings 2:8–15.
3. Job 19:26.

CHAPTER 16: • Let the Word Go Forth!

1. Summit University and ministerial training. An eight-week summer session of Summit University, Levels I and II, was held June 27 through August 25, 1991, at the Royal Teton Ranch. It was sponsored by Lord Maitreya and the World Teachers Jesus and Kuthumi with the Divine Mother and the ascended lady masters. Concurrent with the Summit University session, a six-day ministerial training seminar was conducted August 8 through 13.
2. Three and another three and a seventh. On August 7, 1958, three were present for the dictations of the seven ascended masters who released the

dispensation for The Summit Lighthouse. (See 2008 *Pearls of Wisdom,* vol. 51, nos. 9–15.) In his dictation given that day, Archangel Michael announced that he had begun working with "the lifestreams who shall form the three points of the triangle of Light." He then promised that there would be three others who would "form the three points of a second triangle, making a six-pointed star," and that he would also bring a seventh to "form the physical governing body of this organization."

3. El Morya's diamond and spiritual momentums pledged on the altar. On one occasion, July 3, 1965, El Morya announced that a giant transformer of God's will was being built in the etheric plane to "radiate out to the entire world the good will of Almighty God as an intense and divine holy purpose." El Morya said, "I have taken out the large diamond which I wear in my turban and I have pledged it to the Lords of Creation, that I shall not wear it again until such a time as this activity of this forcefield of good will has accomplished at least 50 percent of the purpose for which it is brought into creation." Thirteen years later, on June 24, 1978, El Morya announced that 50 percent of the purpose to which the transformer was brought forth had been fulfilled. He said, "The Lord God has returned to me the diamond that I had treasured, given to me by my own Guru. . . . You have won for me another opportunity to place the momentum of my causal body upon the altar of humanity." The master also announced that he had established the transformer of God's will congruent with the Ashram of the World Mother in the heart of Los Angeles: "There it shall accomplish, it is my prayer, the balance of its purpose, which is to reinfuse the cities of America and every nation with the momentum from the Great Divine Director's causal body of God-government and the inner blueprint of life." See *Morya: The Darjeeling Master Speaks to His Chelas,* pp. 298, 301–2; 1978 *Pearls of Wisdom,* pp. 297–99 (letter from El Morya); and El Morya, July 4, 1978, available at AscendedMasterLibrary.org. On another occasion, March 24, 1974, against the backdrop of the Watergate investigations, El Morya said: "My turban is flying high and I say, I will unroll it as the scroll and the spiral of that light which God has given me as the diamond. And I place as collateral that diamond of his will upon the altar of God until America is free once again to breathe the fiery air of the Holy Spirit." In a dictation given October 12, 1974, El Morya said, "I stand before you to pledge anew my light and the diamond of my light to Saint Germain, our commander of freedom."
4. El Morya benched and unbenched. In his dictation on August 8, 1988, El Morya announced that there would be no new dispensations for his chelas or for his world service from the Lords of Karma. In short, he was "benched" until karma incurred by dispensations misappropriated or unappropriated by chelas and world servers might be sufficiently balanced. On August 8, 1989, following a year in which the messenger and Keepers of the Flame worldwide joined together in an intense effort to balance this karma through decrees and service, El Morya made the announcement that he was

"unbenched." This, the master said, was by the grace and intercession of Mother Mary and Kuan Yin as well as the extraordinary devotion of the messengers and the chelas. See 1988 *Pearls of Wisdom,* vol. 31, no. 77; 1989 *Pearls of Wisdom,* vol. 32, no. 33.

5. Helios and Vesta's thirty-three-day dispensation. On July 4, 1991, Helios stated: "Now the purposed action of our coming as regards planet Earth is unveiled. . . . For thirty-three days, beloved, we will answer your call. We will answer with the full fire of the Central Sun of Alpha and Omega. We will answer to the fullest extent of the Great Law. If there is something in the world you truly desire to see happen, you can offer a percentage of your causal body, this to be approved by the Lords of Karma." See 1991 *Pearls of Wisdom,* vol. 34, no. 40.
6. Eph. 6:12.
7. Dark Cycle in the physical octave. See *Saint Germain's Prophecy for the Millennium,* pp. 163–69; the release of the karma of the Dark Cycle in the physical octave concluded on April 23, 2002.
8. Acts 8:23.
9. Rev. 3:15, 16.
10. Pruning of the rose bush. In a dictation given May 27, 1984, Elohim Purity and Astrea said: "For the world change that is necessary we demand now the pruning of the rose bush! We demand the pruning of the activity! Let those who understand the mission, the true mission of the bodhisattva, stand up and be counted! And those who do not understand it, let them go their way!" See 1989 *Pearls of Wisdom,* vol. 32, no. 12.
11. Give the decree for binding the dweller-on-the-threshold. See this volume, chapter 14, p. 129, and p. 178–79 note 11.
12. On the cosmic clock, God-reality is charted on the 9 o'clock line under the solar hierarchy of Libra. The perversions of God-reality include dishonesty, intrigue, treachery, and deception. See this volume, chapter 13, p. 176 n. 3.
13. "I Cast Out the Dweller-on-the-Threshold!" decree 20.09, and "I Ratify the Judgment of Helios Whereby the Plug Is Pulled on the Seed of the Wicked," decree 20.12, in *Prayers, Meditations and Dynamic Decrees for Personal and World Transformation.*
14. In Buddhism, the Three Jewels in which the disciple takes refuge (i.e., turns to for protection and aid) are the Buddha, the Dharma, the Sangha. The Buddha is the Enlightened One; the Dharma, the teaching of the Buddha; and the Sangha, the community, the congregation of monks, nuns and lay devotees, the Buddha's spiritual family. The Three Jewels are recited in a verbal formula, or mantra: "I take refuge in the Buddha. I take refuge in the Dharma. I take refuge in the Sangha." See *Maitreya on Initiation,* pp. 108–12; *The Buddhic Essence,* pp. 36–38.
15. Lineage of hierarchy. The order of Gurus in a lineal descent from Sanat Kumara is: Sanat Kumara, Gautama Buddha, Lord Maitreya, Jesus Christ, Padma Sambhava. On July 2, 1977, Padma Sambhava bestowed the mantle

of Guru upon the messenger Elizabeth Clare Prophet. He said: "The ascended masters come as a living witness to proclaim in this hour that the Guru-chela relationship can now be sustained in this octave through the flame of the heart of the Mother." See 1984 *Pearls of Wisdom,* vol. 27, no. 33A, and *Maitreya on Initiation,* pp. 133–35.

16. Luke 22:42; Matt. 26:39; Mark 14:36.
17. Luke 19:20.

CHAPTER 17: • I Deliver the Unconditioned Love

1. Rev. 12:12.
2. The vows of Kuan Yin are included on *Kuan Yin's Crystal Rosary: Devotions to the Divine Mother East and West,* 4 audio CDs, booklet available separately from Store.SummitLighthouse.org. For the messenger's teaching on the vows, see *Maitreya on Initiation,* pp. 112–18.
3. The Buddha, the Dharma (the teaching), and the Sangha (the community) are the Three Jewels of Buddhism. See this volume, chapter 16, p. 181 n. 14.
4. A single virtue to outpicture in this life. At the conclusion of the July 3, 1991 service, the Nameless One from out the Great Central Sun delivered a dictation in which he said that he was placing a seed of light in the crown chakra of "those who will accomplish the path of the mystical union with God in this flesh they now wear." He asked that we embody the name of a virtue and said: "May the name of that virtue become the label on the seed that I have placed that might grow in the crown chakra if you nurture it. May you strive to become the God-identification, the God-embodiment of that virtue. And may you be so, that when you graduate from earth you may be acknowledged for your attainment upon that single virtue. Meditate a moment now and see the title of a single virtue that does descend upon your crown chakra with the seed of light." See 1991 *Pearls of Wisdom,* vol. 34, no. 37.
5. In Buddhism the Dharmakaya, Sambhogakaya, and Nirmanakaya are the three "bodies" of the Buddha. The Dharmakaya corresponds to the upper figure in the Chart of Your Divine Self, the causal body, including the I AM Presence. The Sambhogakaya corresponds to the middle figure—the Holy Christ Self. The Nirmanakaya, defined by Buddhists as the crystallization of the Dharmakaya into human form for the purpose of expounding the teaching and saving other beings, corresponds to the lower figure in the Chart and is employed at the plane of the soul incarnating the I AM.
6. Ezek. 1:4.
7. John 8:23.
8. The Indian scripture *Guru Gita* interprets the Sanskrit word *Guru* to mean "Dispeller of Darkness." (1.44)
9. Acts 9:5; 26:14.

408 pp. ISBN 978-1-60988-355-3

Teachings from the Mystery School

The Maitreya Discourses

ELIZABETH CLARE PROPHET

Come and Find Me . . .

Welcome to the Mystery School of Lord Maitreya—the Buddha of mercy, love and compassion.

Two thousand years ago, Maitreya sent forth the call to his disciple, Jesus, to come and find him. And so Jesus set out for the Himalayas to find the Father, Maitreya, and to receive the teachings that would be the key to an age. Now, once again, Maitreya sends forth the call. Are you one of these fiery spirits that Maitreya Buddha is calling?

Jesus tells us that the Mystery School of Lord Maitreya is "the open door of the coming of the golden age. This is the open door of the pathway of East and West, of the bodhisattvas and the disciples. . . . For once again it may be said that Maitreya is physically present, not as it was in the first Eden but by the extension of ourselves in form through the messenger and the Keepers of the Flame."

Soon after the announcement of the opening of his Mystery School, Lord Maitreya began a series of profound discourses. He asked us to search these teachings and to discover in them the keys to this Age of Maitreya.

In this book you will find those keys to anchoring the consciousness of the Cosmic Christ in your life. Maitreya beckons: "Come and Find Me."

Welcome to the adventure of the ages.

376 pp ISBN 978-1-60988-379-9

Teachings of the Cosmic Christ Volume 1

Restoring the Thread of Contact

ELIZABETH CLARE PROPHET

Teachings from the Mystery School.

In an ancient past—now only recalled in a Biblical account that many think of as legend—man and woman walked and talked with God in the garden of an earthly paradise.

Then came the Fall. We no longer saw the Guru face-to-face. The world became our teacher—the lessons often hard.

Now comes Maitreya—Guru of old. He would open the door of the ancient mystery school once more. But there are requirements to be met before we are ready to enter.

Maitreya would show us the way. The first step: to reestablish the thread of contact with the Guru—and with our own Real Self.

Enter the path of the Cosmic Christ.

Regain the Edenic consciousness.

Find your way back Home.

4 DVDs and 1 MP3 Audio   DVG22004

The Class of the Golden Cycle

Now Is the Time to Become an Adept

ELIZABETH CLARE PROPHET

This album records a moment in cosmic history. On October 14, 1991, the ascended master Saint Germain announced the release of a golden cycle of light from the Great Central Sun. He explained that "this is a spiral . . . that shall affect all evolutions of the Matter cosmos according to the cycle of their individual worlds and planes."

Contains all dictations from The Class of the Golden Cycle conference, plus 3 audio lectures by Elizabeth Clare Prophet ("Karma, Reincarnation and Christianity" excerpt; "A Profile of Ernon, Rai of Suern") and Mark L. Prophet ("Antahkarana, the Web of Life"). A total of over 16 hours of listening and viewing on 4 DVDs and 1 MP3 audio CD.

ABOUT THE SUMMIT LIGHTHOUSE

The Summit Lighthouse is an internationally recognized spiritual center for the advancement of inner awakening. Our international organization is a global family that is inspired, guided, and sponsored by those known as the ascended masters.

The ascended masters are the most beloved and trusted transcendent beings guiding our planet's material and spiritual evolution. Most of the world's religions are currently based on the revelations of one or more of these masters before their ascension. We openly embrace spiritual seekers from all paths of Light including the mystical traditions of the world's religions.

The ascended masters and their messengers have given us over fifteen thousand hours of invaluable inner wisdom and insightful instruction, and they have provided the means for our direct initiation into higher consciousness.

For the ascended masters . . . no subject is off limits! Their teachings contain amazing truths and awesome answers on spirituality, alchemy, astrology, sacred geometry, spiritual science, karma, reincarnation, ascension, archangels (and fallen angels), and even those issues that are considered taboo or "out of this world."

PRIMARY GOALS OF THE TEACHINGS OF THE ASCENDED MASTERS

The ascended masters challenge us daily to be bold, to dare to be who we truly are, and to face adversity with courage, patience, perseverance, honesty, integrity, inner love, discipline, and discernment—all for a greater sense of inner peace, fearlessness, stillness and silence, harmony, self-mastery, compassion, and wisdom.

These teachings help our souls get back to the origin of their individualized inner source of True Self Love—the Higher Self, or I AM Presence. Our point of contact with our Higher Self is the "Spark of Life" or "Sacred Fire of the Heart," the place where our consciousness expresses its true divine nature of unconditional love and happiness, universal oneness, and an authentic desire to serve others.

HOW OUR TEACHINGS CAME INTO BEING

Our teachings were all released through highly trained and trusted messengers, Mark L. Prophet and Elizabeth Clare Prophet. Mark was contacted by the ascended master El Morya at the age of eighteen and received training from him for many years before he was instructed to establish The Summit Lighthouse in 1958 in Washington, D.C.

With his ascension in 1973, Mark passed the torch for the mission to his gifted wife, Elizabeth Clare Prophet, who continued her service until her retirement in 1999.

The dictations of the ascended masters were regularly given in public. The ascended masters also inspired thousands of lectures delivered by the messengers. The content of the dictations are, by most human standards, beyond the mind's ability to construct in real time. They carry very powerful frequencies of light, awakening us to the highest truths we've ever experienced.

We leave it up to you to decide the value for yourself.

MOVING TOWARD YOUR VICTORY

No matter what path of light you are on, spiritual freedom is attained using tools that have been passed down in wisdom teachings through the millennia: meditation, selfless service, devotional music, prayer, mantra, and the science of the spoken Word. The masters bring an accelerated understanding of these principles, especially suited for the challenges of the modern world, including dynamic decree work and the use of the violet flame.

NEXT STEPS

We are genuinely excited to meet you on the path . . . and hope you are too. We extend a warm welcome from everyone at The Summit Lighthouse, and we invite you to explore the teachings of the ascended masters at our website. Check out our free online lessons and hundreds of articles on a wide range of spiritual subjects. Browse through our online bookstore. And if you would rather talk to someone in person, please feel free to contact us today!

Elizabeth Clare Prophet is a world-renowned author, spiritual teacher, and pioneer in practical spirituality. Her groundbreaking books have been published in more than thirty languages and over three million copies have been sold worldwide.

Among her best-selling titles are *The Human Aura; The Science of the Spoken Word; Your Seven Energy Centers; The Lost Years of Jesus; The Art of Practical Spirituality;* and her best-selling Pocket Guides to Practical Spirituality series.

The Summit Lighthouse®
63 Summit Way
Gardiner, Montana 59030 USA

1-800-245-5445 / 406-848-9500

Se habla español.

info@SummitUniversityPress.com
SummitLighthouse.org

9 781609 884260

Printed by Libri Plureos GmbH in Hamburg,
Germany